MW01181194

HELP ME UNDERSTAND
THE BIBLE

CLARENCE WHETSTONE

WESTBOW°
PRESS
A DIVISION OF THOMAS NELSON
& ZONDERVAN

WestBow Press books may be ordered through booksellers or by contacting:

WestBow Press
A Division of Thomas Nelson & Zondervan
1663 Liberty Drive
Bloomington, IN 47403
www.westbowpress.com
1 (866) 928-1240

Because of the dynamic nature of the Internet, any web addresses or links contained in this book may have changed since publication and may no longer be valid. The views expressed in this work are solely those of the author and do not necessarily reflect the views of the publisher, and the publisher hereby disclaims any responsibility for them.

Any people depicted in stock imagery provided by Thinkstock are models, and such images are being used for illustrative purposes only. Certain stock imagery © Thinkstock.

ISBN: 978-1-4908-2719-3 (sc)
ISBN: 978-1-4908-2720-9 (hc)
ISBN: 978-1-4908-2718-6 (e)

Library of Congress Control Number: 2014903500

Printed in the United States of America.

WestBow Press rev. date: 04/16/2014

To Eileen, my wife of many years, my life partner,
my best friend, my love

CONTENTS

ACKNOWLEDGMENTS

First and most important, I must offer reverence to the Father God who called me to himself many years ago, to the Christ who died for my sins, and to the Holy Spirit who guides and comforts me: one God.

I offer my deep appreciation to my parents, the Rev. Clarence Sr. and Helen Koontz Whetstone. They created a home of love and security. They taught me to worship, pray, and revere the Bible as the Word of God.

The Rev. Dr. Ross Whetstone, my only blood brother, deserves my deep appreciation. He has been my spiritual mentor since the time I decided to follow Jesus. I have spent countless hours discussing the things of the Lord with him.

I credit the many individuals and classes I have led in Bible study with forcing me to find answers to the questions they have posed. Their struggle and mine to understand the Bible have motivated this writing. Later, the Holy Spirit pushed me to complete this work.

Edward "Ned" Frear, retired newspaper editor and publisher, graciously offered to critique my efforts. His suggestions were especially valuable.

I must also give deep appreciation to those who read the manuscript and offered their unique criticisms. Nancy Casteel was my target reader. She found many typos and made important suggestions.

Michael Kreiner was selected because he has the unusual viewpoint of a conservative Jew who has accepted Jesus as his Messiah. Cdr. Clay Thomas, US Navy (Ret.), leads a Christian retreat center for US military members. Dr. David Crandall, MD, surgeon and US Army commander (retired) gave valuable medical insights. The Rev. Robert Robertson, active pastor of the First Christian Church, Everett, Pennsylvania, gave me strong encouragement. Finally, Jesse Topper, the executive minister of the Bedford United Methodist Church, gave his unique insights. I offer my sincere thanks to all.

The editorial department of WestBow Press gave me excellent support and encouragement. They are all deeply appreciated.

INTRODUCTION

The primary thrust of this material is the comparison of the Hebrew way versus the Greek way to understand the Bible. Most of us are unaware that we are totally Greek in our thinking. Recognized or not, we look at the world through Greek eyes. We reason the Greek way.

The Greeks developed logic. They loved to define, to sequence, to think in very controlled patterns, and to arrive at conclusions that could not be refuted. We expect to be presented Greek material. When presented with anything else, we try to make Greek out of it. The Greek way of thinking is the only way most of us know. But the Bible is not Greek. It is almost entirely Hebrew.

Many people feel that because the Bible has been translated into their language, all of its problems have been solved. In reality, that is just the first step. There are huge problems with understanding the culture of Bible times. We have big problems understanding the theology of those times. Often, the language of the Bible does not really mean what we expect. Beyond that, ancient thinking patterns are very different from ours.

If I were to present you with a corroded bolt and ask you to remove it with a screwdriver, you would probably tell me that the screwdriver was the wrong tool, and you would be correct. We need a wrench to remove a bolt. In the same way, to solve Hebrew problems we need the correct tools—i.e., Hebrew tools. The Greek tools we know how to use are the wrong ones for Hebrew material, and yet Greek tools are what we almost always use. Most people are not even aware that there is a difference.

The Hebrew Scriptures were written before Greek logic was invented, and yet we expect them to be logical. All the Bible was written before science existed as an academic discipline, and yet we expect the views expressed in the Bible to be scientific. That doesn't make any sense. We need to approach the Bible with the same mind-set as those who wrote it, not with our own, which is so radically different.

Vast problems are created by our not understanding the Hebrew culture and its values. Problems are created by our presuming that we understand their theology. Language presents unique problems. For example, we naturally presume the meaning we know for a word to be the author's intended meaning, when in fact, it often was very different.

My goals are to highlight these problems and suggest solutions for understanding the Bible. We will be considering life's deepest meanings while we are entangled with our patterns of thinking and our often unexamined prejudices. I approach this tangled knot with great humility and with the strongly held belief that Jesus' prayer for the unity of his body on earth, i.e., the Christian church, must be given much higher priority than I have observed during my lifetime. His prayer in John 17 stresses his desire for unity in his church no fewer than four times. If Jesus is our Lord, we should want what he wants.

I am writing for the average reader. Every effort has been made to avoid technical theological terms. Where they are necessary, definitions will be supplied in everyday language.

The sections that make up this book progress from the most understandable to the most difficult material: the topic of Hebrew thought. This last material will require the greatest effort on the part of the reader. However, once understood, I believe it will be of the greatest value.

Why do I feel qualified to wrestle with this material? I was immersed in the Bible from my mother's knee. I grew up in a parsonage family and was required to attend Sunday school, worship, Bible studies, Bible conferences, etc., all my life. The Bible has been my primary source of study for all of my adult life. Being expected to become a pastor, I started to train for it. I was licensed as a local pastor and led three small congregations for three years while in college. One year of theological seminary followed before I left the ministerial training track.

During a total of nine and a half years of higher education, I amassed four majors of thirty-plus hours each: English, theology, psychology, and speech therapy. For at least the past thirty years, I have been writing my own Sunday school material for both youth and adults.

Finally, I felt compelled by the Holy Spirit to write this material. I share it, expecting that there are others who have had the same questions that I wrestled with for so many years. Let's take a journey together, thinking through this problem of understanding the Bible.

PART I

READING THE BIBLE

CHAPTER 1

HOW DO I APPROACH THE BIBLE?

"Do you know anyone who doesn't believe the Bible?" Jody asked.

"Oh, sure. Lots of guys at school make fun of it," Phil replied.

"But, do you believe it? Jody continued.

"Yes, I've been taught to believe it. But, there sure is a lot I don't understand," Phil answered.

When I was a teenager, I knew of an old German butcher who read his Bible more than most Christians. But he did not read it *devotionally*. He was a nonbeliever and felt that believers were stupid to believe it. He read his Bible so he could argue with his customers and try to prove them wrong. To him, the Bible was a closed book. He simply could not understand it.

Practically everyone approaches the Bible with an idea of what it is:

> a dusty old book
> the mythology of the early Christians
> the manual for seed faith
> a source of division within modern society
> the manual for claiming God's promises
> illogical ramblings of the past
> the written Word of God

Can we see that the position we take *before* we open the Bible will affect what we find in it? People tend to find what they are looking for! Dallas Willard wrote: "Our preexisting ideas and assumptions are precisely what we can see, hear or otherwise observe."[1] If we discount the Bible even before we begin to read it, we are not apt to see the truth there. Satan has won the battle, for our Christian source material has been neutralized!

If we think of the Bible as irrelevant, out of date, or divisive, we will pay little attention to it. Many who ignore the Bible do not really know what's there! R. C. Sproul wrote: "Isn't it amazing that almost everyone living in the West has an opinion to offer about the Bible, and yet so few have really studied it?"[2] Other things are more important—getting to work, the morning paper, that trip we want to take, or even a cup of coffee.

On the other hand, if we really believe the Bible to be the written Word of God, it is *the* source of information about our Creator and what he wants from us. Only our response to God could be as important!

Let's suppose that I have been infected with the philosophical virus very common in our culture—the one that says the Bible does not relate to our modern times. What can I do?

First, I must become aware of my mind-set. Television psychologist Dr. Phil McGraw often says that we cannot change what we do not acknowledge. Okay, then what is my mind-set toward the Bible? Am I viewing it as the written Word of God or in some other way?

Second, I need to *ask God to open my mind to his truth*. If I think I have all the answers, why would I need to look any further? Martin Luther wrote in the 1400–1500s: "Where the Spirit does not open the scripture, the scripture is not understood, even though it is read."[3] A. W. Tozer wrote: "The unbelieving mind would not be convinced by any proof, and the worshipping heart needs none."[4] To be aware of God, love God, and serve God, I need to be open to *his truth*.

Third, I need to learn to know Jesus as the firsthand teacher sent from God to show us what God is like. So I need to read the Gospels (Matthew, Mark, Luke, and John) over and over, until I know Jesus *extremely well*—as well as I know my brother or sister.

Fourth, I must honestly consider the claims that Jesus lays on my life. Is he who he says he is? Did he really come from heaven? Did he really come to save me from my sins? Am I willing to accept him as my Savior and Lord of my life? If I say yes to Jesus, the Bible will suddenly change from being irrelevant to being the most important information I can find. It will become for me the written Word of God.

Most people seem to feel that their problems understanding the Bible come from *within* the Bible. This chapter stresses that at least part of the problem lies within us! The doubting brain ignores inconvenient truth—even God's truth!

One more step will make the Bible even more relevant to us than it is now. We must learn to read the Bible through Hebrew eyes. Why? The Bible was written from their culture and in their time.

By approaching the Bible with American or Western eyes, we miss so much. We miss its beauty. We miss its life-shattering power. And we often misinterpret the words of Jesus and the prophets.

It never occurs to most of us that the Bible is in many respects a foreign book. We get along with it quite well—we think. After all, in the Bible we meet the God of creation and discover that he is a God who loves us. We meet Jesus as the carpenter/teacher who reached out to the poor and needy—and we like him. Then we hear that Jesus died so that our sins can be forgiven. Whoopee! We hear about the Holy Spirit who will enable us to live lives beyond our own abilities–and we like that too. What more do we need?

I think it is nothing short of amazing that we can take material like the Bible, transplant it to another radically different culture, and find that it still works! Lives are still changed. Sin and bitterness are still lifted. Forgiveness and healing still flow from its pages. Hope for a better day is instilled. And love at a sacrificial level is demonstrated.

But the Bible *is* a foreign book. It did not come from the pen of Plato or Socrates. It is not the product of the thinking of Western philosophers. Freud and other psychologists had nothing to do with its writing. As great as Shakespeare was as a writer, nothing in his work can compare. Even Mark Twain's wit and philosophy doesn't make the grade. These heroes of the West were great thinkers who, here and there, were given bits of truth, but their work never leads to a relationship with the Creator!

We have acted as if we in the West know all truth. But God chose to bring the truth of his nature and purpose to us *through people we barely understand*!

In summary, the simple person will find life-changing truth in the Bible. The scholar will find the same life-changing truth—and layer after layer of exquisite truths intertwined in ways that boggle the human mind. To really understand the Bible requires a lifetime of devoted scholarship. Unlike other books, the message of the Bible has layers of meaning. It can be read for the obvious surface meaning. It can be read for deeper spiritual meanings. It can also be seen as allegory, where every person or action relates to our real lives.

William Law of the 1600-1700s wrote: "When in reading scripture you meet with a passage that seems to give your heart a new motion towards God, turn it into the form of a petition, and give it a place in your prayers."[5] The Bible can even be the avenue that forms your prayers.

The heart and mind devoted to God will find an endless banquet table in the Bible.

CHAPTER 2

WHERE DO I START READING?

"Can you stick to reading your Bible every day like the pastor wants?" asked Jody.

"I'm trying," replied Phil. "But I have to admit, it's like taking my vitamins. Sometimes I forget."

This reminds me of a story. Mike was sitting in his easy chair, reading a very large book. His wife walked in and was surprised to see Mike reading anything beyond the comics in the newspaper. "Good for you," she said. "I told you that reading was good for your brain."

"Maybe so," he replied, "but so far I can't figure out what this story means."

"What are you reading?" she asked as she picked the book out of his hands. "My collection of old poetry?"

Obviously, a collection of poetry has no plot. In the same way, the Bible is not a novel. It is a small library, a collection of writings, an anthology.

Certainly you can start reading an anthology at the beginning, because you don't have any better starting place. But because so many people get stuck in the Old Testament and stop reading, I urge you to choose a better starting place and a better sequence for reading.

The heart of the Bible is Jesus. Therefore, you should first get to know Jesus as well as you know your best friend. You will find him in the Gospels: Matthew, Mark, Luke, and John. Start there. I strongly suggest that you read the gospels over and over and over, until you are saturated with Jesus.

These four Gospels give different viewpoints of Jesus' life. Matthew, Mark, and Luke are very Hebrew. John is very Greek but was written from a Hebrew mind-set. Maybe you would like to start with John, because we also have a very Greek orientation. You can buy the gospel of John in a small, single volume and carry it in your pocket to read at any spare moment, or you can put it on your smartphone. At any rate, don't move from the Gospels until you have read them over and over and you feel you know Jesus intimately. Don't quit the Gospels until you can always tell what is going to happen next.

Then turn to Acts (formerly called the Acts of the Apostles). This details the initial and then explosive growth of the early church. I wouldn't be surprised if you developed a deep desire for a closer life with God as you read these accounts.

After that, read through the rest of the New Testament, Romans through Jude, to see the early church with its problems and how God repeatedly corrected it. I am going to recommend that you *not* try Revelation until you've gone through the Old Testament—which you will only be ready to read after you know the New Testament inside and out.

As you read the Old Testament you will begin to understand that it is the foundation for the New Testament. *The Old Testament cannot be discarded!* In it we see God creating and developing his relationship to humanity. We find the Ten Commandments, which are still God's law for good living (Exodus 20). We see God setting up the sacrifice system for the covering of the people's sins, and his repeatedly reaching out to his people through the prophets. We feel the heart of God for lost foreigners (as in Jonah) and his love for his chosen people (as in Hosea). We see flashes of the coming Messiah (as in Psalm 22 and Isaiah 53). And throughout, we find the amazing promises of a Messiah that is to come to save his people.

The Old Testament (old covenant) records the repeated failures of God's people to keep their side of the agreement with God. The apostle Paul refers to the old covenant (the law) as a schoolmaster that showed the people their inability to keep God's law and, consequently, their need for the Messiah. "Let me put it another way. The law was our guardian until Christ came; it protected us until we could be made right with God through faith. And now that the way of faith has come, we no longer need the law as our guardian." (Gal. 3:24–25 NLT).

The New Testament (new covenant) records God coming to earth in human form as Jesus of Nazareth. Jesus taught of a new relationship with God—a relationship of the heart, not a keeping of external rules. Jesus called this the kingdom of God, where God is the King of each life that receives him. The writer of Hebrews said it this way: "This is the covenant I will make with the house of Israel after that time, declares the Lord. I will put my laws in their minds and write them on their hearts. I will be their God, and they will be my people." (Heb. 8:10 NIV).

So, it is important to master the New Testament before turning to the Old Testament. You will find treasures in the Old Testament that make sense, once the New Testament is fully understood.

Finally, I recommend a quick read-through of the New Testament again. Then we can turn to the last book, which is considered more fully in the last chapter of this book.

Obviously, reading the Bible this way will not be easy. The Bible is so deep, so rich, that it is unlike other books. R. C. Sproul wrote: "There is no room for reading once-over-lightly in our study of Scripture. Knowing Scripture is a life-long project which requires diligence and perseverance."[1]

The benefits are well worth your effort!

So, start with Jesus. He is the heart of the Bible, including Revelation. Jesus came to reveal the Father to us. Learn to know him as a best friend. Then allow his Holy Spirit to guide you as he leads you into deeper truth.

PART II

PROBLEMS UNDERSTANDING HEBREW CULTURE

CHAPTER 3

WHO IS THIS WOMAN AT THE WELL?

Jody and Phil were talking about the church service they'd just left.

"What's the big deal about Jesus talking with that Samaritan woman at the well?" Phil asked. "We're supposed to be kind and helpful. I don't get it."

The account of Jesus' encounter with the Samaritan woman is found in John 4:4–42. Since this passage is so long, let me summarize it for you. Jesus and his disciples were walking through Samaria. They stopped at Jacob's well. While Jesus was resting there, a woman of Samaria came to draw water. Jesus engaged her in conversation. After a lengthy discussion Jesus identified himself as the Messiah. She then ran to tell the villagers that she had found the Promised One. From our American point of view, this looks like a normal, everyday event. But from their point of view, it was dangerous and unacceptable.

What don't we understand?

First of all, in America today we expect equality between the sexes. We expect that a woman would be treated as an equal. But was that the case there and then? The difference is significant! Males were in charge; females were property. Men made the decisions; women were expected to obey. Men sat as judges at the city gates; women went to men for justice. Men owned land and property; women owned only a little dowry of coins and the clothing on their backs. Boys went to school; girls stayed home to learn from their mothers. Men went out to work; women stayed home to have and care for babies. This arrangement is called *patriarchal*—i.e., males were in charge. The Samaritan woman expected to be treated as property. She was used to being kicked around. In that culture, she was not really a person. She was an object.

Our understanding of this account is also challenged because we think of divorce in terms of equality as well. We feel that either party can file for divorce, leave a bad marriage, and go on with life. By contract, the Samaritan woman had almost no rights. Remember, she was property. She could not file for divorce, no matter what. But her husband could divorce her at any point, for any reason. If he found a prettier face, a better cook, or a woman who was in any way a better marriage partner, he could simply give his wife a note saying that she was divorced, and she was gone. She had no recourse. A woman usually had no skills with which to support herself. She was expected to be under the "protection" of a male—her father, brother, or husband.

The Samaritan woman was not officially under any protection, because she was no longer married. She had, in fact, been thrown out of five marriages. How is that for rejection? Somehow she had found food and shelter with another man, but even he would not give her the security of his name. They were just "shacking up."

Another cultural difference that we need to understand in order to fully grasp just how profoundly unique was Jesus' behavior toward this woman is this: the social separation of the sexes was treated severely. A male was not to so much as look a woman in the eye, let alone talk to her. As she approached the well, Jesus was expected to get up and move at least twenty-five feet away. She had to draw water, but he was expected to ignore her. She was just a woman, unworthy of his time. Even the women of her town scorned her. They came to the well in the cool of the morning or evening. To avoid the ridicule of the other women of town, she came to the well during the heat of the day.

In addition to being the object of scorn because of her marital status, this woman was from an apostate nation. Samaritans were half-breeds, part Hebrew and part Canaanite, Syrian, or Phoenician. They had intermarried and brought foreign idols and foreign worship into the Hebrew way of life. This was false, or apostate, worship. All Hebrews were to totally shun all Samaritans. If a Hebrew and a Samaritan crossed paths, the Hebrew pretended that the Samaritan was invisible.

Jesus' culture identified this woman as more than apostate. She was the enemy. Over the years, there had been cross-border raids from both sides. Each nation hated the other. Jesus was expected to hate her.

Add up the negatives. She was female, rejected from five marriages, and "shacking up." She was property, a member of the enemy nation, a half-breed, and an apostate. She was as insignificant, unworthy, despised, and hated as one can imagine. Jesus was supposed to ignore her existence. Instead, he talked to her.

Is it any wonder she was shocked? A *man* was talking to her *in public.* She recognized immediately, by both dress and accent, that he was a

Hebrew—the enemy. Everything about her past must have made her think, *Here is another man trying to use me.* Maybe it was his tone of voice, his eyes, or his expression, but instead of leaving, she engaged in conversation with him. He didn't look down on her. He treated her with dignity. Had she ever been treated with dignity before? How wonderful it was to be treated as a person of worth!

She had a quick mind and asked valid questions. Finally she said, "I know that when the Messiah comes, he will tell us all things."

Jesus answered, "I am the Messiah."

His answer must have staggered her. *The Messiah … here? Now? Talking to me?* But she didn't waffle about indecisively. She left her water pot and ran—back to the village, back to the people who had scorned and abused her. "Come, see a man who knows all about me. Could this be the Messiah?"

You see, this is a big deal. From an American perspective, a man talking to a woman at a well looks normal. But once we understand the culture, we can see that it was anything but normal. It was, in fact, an explosive situation. Jesus was in enemy territory. They hated him, and he was expected to hate everybody there. Instead of doing what was expected, Jesus cared enough to minister to a hurting soul—and later, to many hurting souls.

Jesus broke down the walls of separation their culture had built. He gave the Samaritan woman acceptance and worth. She responded immediately by risking more scorn as she spread the message. She became the first foreign missionary of Christianity. How's that for irony?

You may wonder how people could treat all women that way. How could they be so insensitive? But this was not just an Israeli/Samaritan problem. All of the Middle East was like that. It was "just the way it was!" I suppose, because of their larger frames and muscle mass, males were able to control females. And the desire to control others is as old as playing "king of the hill."

We cannot be too self-righteous about sexual equality. In the United States, women did not have the right to vote or hold office until the Nineteenth Amendment passed in 1920 after an extensive and hard-fought campaign.

The effect of Jesus' actions against this discrimination will be shown in a later chapter. If you understand that the Middle Eastern culture placed all women in roles inferior to men, it will help you understand the Bible. There were a few outstanding women who were able to rise above the restrictions of the culture. I suppose they were unusually intelligent and/or extremely beautiful. But most women were held in the position of property.

Yes, Jesus talking to a Samaritan woman was a big deal. Talking to her as a person of worth was a big deal. In that encounter, Jesus was planting seeds of sexual equality. Like a root pressing through a crack, those seeds slowly broke the rock of oppression.

CHAPTER 4

WHY SHOULD I CARE ABOUT MARY AND MARTHA?

Jody and Phil were chatting. "I don't get why Martha was so bent out of shape," Phil said. "Someone should have visited with Jesus while Martha was getting the meal on."

"Maybe she needed help," Jody suggested. "I don't know."

Let's look at the whole event.

As Jesus and his disciples were on their way, he came to a village where a woman named Martha opened her home to him. She had a sister called Mary, who sat at the Lord's feet listening to what he said. But Martha was distracted by all the preparations that had to be made. She came to him and asked, "Lord, don't you care that my sister has left me to do the work by myself? Tell her to help me!"¶ "Martha," the Lord answered, "you are worried and upset about many things, but only one thing is needed. Mary has chosen what is better, and it will not be taken away from her." (Luke 10:38–42 NIV)

To us this looks like sibling rivalry. Martha wanted Mary to help her in the kitchen, and Mary was getting out of the work by entertaining their guest. But we don't get the real issue.

In chapter one, we referred to male/female roles in that culture. Remember that only boys went to school. Girls stayed home to learn housekeeping and cooking. Boys went to the synagogue to learn from the teacher of the Law. The boys' role at school was primarily to memorize the Torah, the first five books of the Bible. They were to learn the Law of God. The teacher sat in the "seat of Moses." The boys sat on the floor and repeated for memorization what the teacher read from the scroll.

Girls were not to be concerned with such things. They were to concentrate on carrying water, gathering wood, cooking and keeping house, and caring for the smaller children.

Mary was breaking the barrier. She was sitting at Jesus' feet, listening to his teaching. *That was a boy's task.* She was not supposed to be concerned about the teachings of Jesus. She was supposed to be in a female role, preparing and serving food.

What did Jesus say about Martha's request for help? He said that Mary had chosen the *better thing.* What was that better thing? It was listening to and learning Jesus' teachings.

Can you see that Jesus was breaking the social structure? Girls were supposed to know their place. But Jesus was saying that *his teachings were more important than the social fabric of that time and place.*

This little cameo is powerful. Jesus was planting a seed that took centuries to come to full bloom. But when it came to bloom, women were able to study and hold office alongside men.

It is almost certain that Jesus invited Mary to learn from him. It would have been extremely presumptuous of Mary to have asked Jesus to break the social fabric. Apparently Jesus saw in Mary a spirit that was hungry for the things of God. Jesus always responded to an open and searching spirit. Now females too could study the Law of God. It was not a male-only thing.

No wonder the establishment felt threatened by Jesus and responded negatively: "Next thing you know, these girls are going to get uppity. They're going to want more and more. The day is coming when they are going to want to be judges at the city gates. We have to keep people in their place."

In this scene, Jesus was *again* disturbing the social order. Order is a good thing—better than anarchy. But order that suppresses people, not allowing them to develop the skills and talents that God has given them, is not God's plan. This is a repressive order, much like racism. Jesus did not campaign against it; he had a much larger task at hand. But he did demonstrate by his actions what God wants from his people.

In America we expect to be able to climb out of our situations. That is the American dream. But in Bible times, the people felt that their positions were quite fixed. God made some notable exceptions to that: calling Saul from the bottom of the line to become king, for example.

When you realize the very fixed social order imposed on people of the Middle Eastern culture, this will help you understand the Bible.

CHAPTER 5

WOULD JESUS TALK
TO THE ENEMY?

"What is a centurion, anyway?" Jody asked. "I wish the Bible would use words that I know."

"I don't know," Phil replied. "It sounds like 'century.' That's a hundred years, isn't it?"

"Well, a hundred years doesn't make sense either," Jody answered. "It's all Greek to me."

Here is more confusion that comes from differences in culture. First, let's read the account of this centurion in Matthew.

When Jesus had entered Capernaum, a centurion came to him, asking for help. "Lord," he said, "my servant lies at home paralyzed and in terrible suffering."¶ Jesus said to him, "I will go and heal him."¶ The centurion replied, "Lord, I do not deserve to have you come under my roof. But just say the word, and my servant will be healed. For I myself am a man under authority, with soldiers under me. I tell this one, 'Go,' and he goes; and that one, 'Come,' and he comes. I say to my servant, 'Do this,' and he does it."¶ When Jesus heard this, he was astonished and said to those following him, "I tell you the truth, I have not found anyone in Israel with such great faith. I say to you that many will come from the east and the west, and will take their places at the feast with Abraham, Isaac and Jacob in the kingdom of heaven. But the subjects of the kingdom will be thrown outside, into the darkness, where there will be weeping and gnashing of teeth."¶ Then Jesus said to the centurion, "Go! It will be done just as you believed it would." And his servant was healed at that very hour." (Matt. 8:5–13 NIV)

What kind of person is coming to Jesus for assistance?

The International Standard Bible Encyclopedia defines him this way: "As the name implies, … [a centurion] was the commander of a hundred men, more or less, in a Roman legion … The ordinary duties of the centurion were to drill his men, inspect their arms, food and clothing, and to command them in the camp and in the field."[1]

So, this man was an officer of the Roman army. Immediately, you should be able to feel the tension in this situation. This man was not only an officer, but he was an *enemy* officer. He represented the occupying power—brutal, tyrannical, Roman power.

Most of us are very sensitive to figures of authority: police, military, and so on. I am sure the disciples became very apprehensive as this centurion approached them. Were his intentions good or bad? The disciples knew better than to object. This man had the power of Rome behind him, and they were a conquered people.

But this commanding officer was coming to Jesus. The commander was requesting something from a subject! Why?

He was approaching because he had heard of or seen Jesus teaching, healing, and ministering to the common people. He recognized that Jesus had power that even Rome didn't have. Isn't that amazing? The political and military power that could conquer the world could not heal a suffering person. Rome could destroy, but Rome could not heal.

Notice first that this centurion said he was not worthy of Jesus coming into his house. The centurion was placing Jesus above himself, placing Jesus in the position of authority and power. He clearly saw Jesus at least as a prophet with divine power—power that the world's military ruler did not have.

Jesus immediately indicated that he would go with the centurion—even though Hebrews were not to go into Gentile house and heal the servant. But the centurion disagreed. "All you have to do is say the word. I understand authority. If you say it, it is done."

Jesus was astonished at his understanding. This centurion functioned in a military organization, but he understood lines of spiritual authority too. Obviously, Jesus had divine power that did not require his presence. He simply had to say the word—and he did. Jesus could not have been forced to heal anyone. He *chose* to heal the servant of the enemy.

To understand the culture of the Bible, we have to recognize that the Hebrews were a conquered people. They lived under the heavy heel of Roman authority.

Even Jesus' teaching about carrying a load for a mile is related to that oppression. "If someone forces you to go one mile, go with him two miles" (Matt. 5:41 NIV).

Who could force a Jew to go with him for a mile? Any Roman soldier could.

William Barclay wrote: "At any moment a Jew might feel the touch of the flat of a Roman spear on his shoulder, and know that he was compelled to serve the Romans, it might be in the most menial way. That, in fact, is what happened to Simon of Cyrene, when he was compelled to bear the cross of Jesus."[2]

Conquered and oppressed, the Jews longed desperately for the days of David and Solomon when they had been free and blessed. All of the years we read about in the gospels and in Acts were lived under this oppression, and the people desperately wanted to be free again.

While reading the New Testament, you have to remember that all of the area we call the "Bible lands" were under the brutal control of a foreign power—Rome.

CHAPTER 6

WOULD JESUS APPROVE A COLLABORATOR?

"Being a tax collector is no worse than being a doctor or a truck driver," Jody insisted. "I don't understand all the fuss about Zacchaeus being a tax collector."

"Maybe he was crooked or something—you know, on the take," Phil responded.

"Well, yeah, maybe," Jody said. "I don't know."

Let's first read the account.

Jesus entered Jericho and was passing through. A man was there by the name of Zacchaeus; he was a chief tax collector and was wealthy. He wanted to see who Jesus was, but being a short man he could not, because of the crowd. So he ran ahead and climbed a sycamore-fig tree to see him, since Jesus was coming that way.¶ When Jesus reached the spot, he looked up and said to him, "Zacchaeus, come down immediately. I must stay at your house today." 6 So he came down at once and welcomed him gladly.¶ All the people saw this and began to mutter, "He has gone to be the guest of a 'sinner.'"¶ But Zacchaeus stood up and said to the Lord, "Look, Lord! Here and now I give half of my possessions to the poor, and if I have cheated anybody out of anything, I will pay back four times the amount."¶ Jesus said to him, "Today salvation has come to this house, because this man, too, is a son of Abraham. For the Son of Man came to seek and to save what was lost." (Luke 19:1-10 NIV)

In America, Jody is right. Being a tax collector is to hold an honorable position. Such a person certainly has to be reliable in handling huge amounts of civic money. But that understanding cannot be transferred to the New Testament. Several pieces of information about that culture must be grasped in order to understand the Bible.

Galilee, Samaria, and Judea were conquered nations at the time of Jesus. The Roman general Pompey seized control of the area in 63 BC. The Roman army was garrisoned at the corner of the temple mount. Herod the Great ruled and was an effective tyrant for Rome. He kept those restless people under control, severely putting down any and every hint of breaking free from Rome.

Galilee and Judea, as occupied countries, were taxed very heavily. Life was hard at best. The temple required a tithe of 10 percent for its function and maintenance, and there were numerous other smaller taxes. But the biggest one came when Rome sent word to its collectors that they needed a specific sum for roads, aqueducts, or stadia. These cost untold millions in our money. It was the tax collector's job to squeeze the money out of the people.

The chief tax collector had won the right to his job by outbidding his competition. He needed to get Rome's money, his bid money, and his personal wage—and often much more, if possible, for himself—from the people by leaning on them. Of course, he had the power of the Roman army to back up his demands. He could force them to sell land, cattle, or even their children. Naturally, the people feared and hated him.

They would have been afraid of the tax collector if he had been a Roman. But this was worse. This man was a fellow countryman. He had turned against his own people to make money for himself. In their minds, he was a traitor in their midst.

But we are not done yet. The tax money squeezed out of the people's misery was being used to declare Caesar as God. Annually, each adult had to pledge allegiance to Caesar by burning a pinch of incense in the public square and saying, "Caesar is Lord." This was a political move done to unify the empire. Orthodox Hebrews considered this blasphemy, because only Jehovah was Lord. They felt they were being forced to deny their faith in the one and only true God.

What kind of person would be willing to join the enemy, turn on his neighbors, and profit by their misery? A man like Zacchaeus. He was a blasphemer, a traitor, and a thief. *Despicable* is not a harsh enough word for him.

Then Jesus came into view. As always, there was a swarm of people around Jesus, straining to catch every word, wanting his touch, hoping for his blessing.

Suddenly, Jesus stopped. He looked up into the sycamore fig tree. There was Zacchaeus, straining to see Jesus, his eagerness showing his openness to the message. Jesus even knew his name. Then Jesus did what was not politically correct. He invited himself for dinner at the home of Zacchaeus.

With the approval that Jesus had just given him, Zacchaeus knew it was safe to climb down from the tree. We can be very sure that the only friends Zacchaeus had were fellow collaborators. He hurriedly took Jesus to his home and collected his friends for a feast—a lavish one, to be sure. Zacchaeus had to show his hospitality.

From our American point of view, we miss the impact of Zacchaeus' statement. "But Zacchaeus stood up and said to the Lord, 'Look, Lord! Here and now I give half of my possessions to the poor, and if I have cheated anybody out of anything, I will pay back four times the amount'" (Luke 19:8 NIV).

Craig S. Keener, PhD, professor of New Testament Studies and Christian Origins, says, "In ancient accounts of discipleship, a radical response with possessions was a certain sign of newly acquired devotion to the teacher."[1]

Oh! Zacchaeus was saying he would prove that he was now a disciple of Jesus by his generous giving to the poor and 400 percent returned to anyone he had defrauded. He was saying, "Jesus is now the Lord of my life, and I will prove it by giving away huge amounts of money." Let's suppose he was a millionaire. He had just said that he would give half a million to the poor and a 400 percent return to anybody he had overcharged. How is that for putting your money where your mouth is?

Proof of following Jesus *is* in the way we live life.

Did Jesus approve Zacchaeus? Yes, Jesus loved even a despised collaborator!

CHAPTER 7

WAS IT PUNISHMENT OR TERRORISM?

"I don't like to see torture," Jody said. "Do you?"

"No, I turn to other stuff right away," replied Phil. "Lots of people must like it, though. There's plenty of violence all over the screen."

Jody and Phil would have needed tough stomachs to survive in Bible times. Life was severe back then. The most terrible form of torture known was crucifixion, the way Jesus died.

Much of my information that follows came from a presentation in the 1970s by Dr. Robert Greenawalt, MD, a physician in the Chambersburg, Pennsylvania, area. He and his daughter were both medical doctors who made an extensive study of the medical aspects of crucifixion. (Certainly Dr. Greenawalt has graduated to glory by now.)

First, Jesus was bound and taken for an illegal nighttime trial. "They bound him, led him away and handed him over to Pilate, the governor." (Matt. 27:2 NIV).

Can you imagine how any of us would have reacted to that? We would have been screaming, "You can't do this. This is illegal!" It *was* illegal, but Jesus went quietly.

Pilate's primary concern was to keep peace in this always-ready-to-explode territory. His first allegiance was to Rome, which had placed him as governor of the area. His job was to keep the lid on this boiling cauldron. "But he had Jesus flogged, and handed him over to be crucified." (Matt. 27:26b NIV).

The word *flogged* has no meaning to the average American. My dictionary uses the word *scourged* for the same thing. *The IVP Bible Background Commentary* defines it this way. "Crucifixion was prefaced by scourging, either on the way to the cross or before the victim began the trip to the cross. Tied to a post, the condemned person would be beaten with the *flagellum:* a leather whip with metal knotted into its thongs. This whipping bloodied the victim's back, leaving strips of flesh hanging from the wounds. By weakening the victim's constitution, it would mercifully shorten the time it would take the condemned person to die on the cross."[1]

Next, Jesus was taken to King Herod. There he was made fun of as the Hebrew leaders continued to falsely accuse him. Can you put yourself in his place and experience how it felt to be lied about and made sport of? They were experts in breaking people's spirits. "Then Herod and his soldiers ridiculed and mocked him. Dressing him in an elegant robe, they sent him back to Pilate." (Luke 23:11–12 NIV). Not finding anything about which he could take legal action, Herod sent Jesus back to Pilate.

"They stripped him and put a scarlet robe on him, and then twisted together a crown of thorns and set it on his head. They put a staff in his right hand and knelt in front of him and mocked him. "Hail, king of the Jews!" they said. They spit on him, and took the staff and struck him on the head again and again. After they had mocked him, they took off the robe and put his own clothes on him. Then they led him away to crucify him." (Matt. 27:28–31 NIV).

Here Jesus was mocked even more severely. They pretended to kneel in submission before him. He was given a crown, but not of gold. It was of thorns. They took his staff, a symbol of authority, and beat the thorns into his head. Spitting on him was the ultimate insult to that authority.

By this point, Jesus was very bloody from the scourging, the crown of thorns, and the pulling out of his beard. Now he had to carry the beam of his cross to the place of crucifixion. This strong carpenter/mason had been so weakened by the events that he stumbled under the burden. Simon of Cyrene was assigned the duty of carrying it.

At Golgotha (Calvary), soldiers laid Jesus on the crossbeam and nailed his arms to it. Nails in the palm, as we often see pictured, would not have carried his body weight. They had to be placed in the wrist. The Hebrew description of nail placement is not as accurate as we Greeks would like. We clearly distinguish between the hand and the wrist. Their description of the wrist is less accurate than ours.

The executioners used rope to pull up the crossbeam bearing the crucified one and dropped it into the slot of an already placed upright post. Then they drove a nail through both feet. The weight of the body pulled down on the hands/wrists, causing unbearable pain.

I recently experienced the pain of a damaged ulnar nerve,[2] which enervates the little finger and the one next to it. The pain was so severe that prescribed narcotics only slightly dulled it. There was no relief until after surgery. The pain was horrible. I can't imagine the pain of a spike through the wrist. I recently read that the pain of crucifixion was so severe that a new word had to be created for it: *excruciating.*

Beyond the crucifixion itself, there was also pain from the flogging, the thorns, and the torn beard. But terrible as the pain was, that was not what killed the condemned.

Infection developed from all the wounds, which quickly led to a severe fever. But that was not what killed the condemned, either.

Death came from suffocation. In the position of crucifixion, with the weight of the body on the wrist nails, the condemned could not get an adequate breath. Becoming short of breath, the only thing one could do was to push up on the nails in the feet, which would add to the pain there. Because the person could not get a good breath, the heart raced, trying to get more oxygen to the brain. This cycle repeated continuously, finally leading to heart failure—and death.

This was why the Roman soldiers broke the legs of the other two men who were crucified with Jesus. They wanted to prevent them from being able to push up to get more breath. Lacking that breath, the condemned would die more quickly. "But when they came to Jesus and found that he was already dead, they did not break his legs. Instead, one of the soldiers pierced Jesus' side with a spear, bringing a sudden flow of blood and water (John 19:33–35 NIV).

"About the ninth hour Jesus cried out in a loud voice, *'Eloi, Eloi, lama sabachthani?'*—which means, 'My God, my God, why have you forsaken me?'" (Matt. 27:46 NIV). Jesus had always had perfect fellowship with the Father. Now, as he carried the sins of the world, a terrible, awful, ugly burden, the Father turned from him. Jesus was alone for the first time in his existence. *Our sins broke his heart.*

The cross was not a clean, private death. It was dirty, public, and horrible. William Barclay wrote: "When the Roman general, Varus, had broken the revolt of Judas of Galilee, he crucified two thousand Jews, and placed the crosses by the wayside along the roads to Galilee."[3] Not only were their deaths horrible, but these poor souls did not even get a burial. The birds picked the rotting flesh from their bones until their bodies fell from the crosses, and then the vermin and insects cleaned the bones.

How terrible! That was exactly the response Rome was trying to get. The cross was a deliberate act on the part of the conqueror to *terrorize the victims into compliance with Rome's commands.* Rome was demonstrating its policy: if you do not obey, you will die a horrible death just like that. Terrorism is not new.

To understand the Bible, we have to try to feel the oppression these people constantly lived under in the New Testament.

"Oh, God. Hear your people's cries."

CHAPTER 8

WAS HUMAN LIFE THAT CHEAP?

"*Eunuch?* What in the world is that?" asked Jody. "I'm not even sure I know how to say it."

"I've never heard of it either," said Phil. "Let's ask the pastor."

Let's begin with the Bible account.

Now an angel of the Lord said to Philip, "Go south to the road— the desert road—that goes down from Jerusalem to Gaza." So he started out, and on his way he met an Ethiopian *eunuch*, an important official in charge of all the treasury of Candace, queen of the Ethiopians. This man had gone to Jerusalem to worship, and on his way home was sitting in his chariot reading the book of Isaiah the prophet. The Spirit told Philip, "Go to that chariot and stay near it." ¶ Then Philip ran up to the chariot and heard the man reading Isaiah the prophet. "Do you understand what you are reading?" Philip asked. ¶ "How can I," he said, "unless someone explains it to me?" So he invited Philip to come up and sit with him. ¶ The *eunuch* was reading this passage of Scripture: "He was led like a sheep to the slaughter, and as a lamb before the shearer is silent, so he did not open his mouth. In his humiliation he was deprived of justice. Who can speak of his descendants? For his life was taken from the earth." ¶ The *eunuch* asked Philip, "Tell me, please, who is the prophet talking about, himself or someone else?" Then Philip began with that very passage of Scripture and told him the good news about Jesus. ¶ As they traveled along the road, they came to some water and the *eunuch* said, "Look, here is water. Why shouldn't I be baptized?" And he gave orders to stop the chariot. Then both Philip and the *eunuch* went down into the water and Philip baptized him. When they came up out of the water, the Spirit of the Lord suddenly took Philip away, and the *eunuch* did not see him again, but went on his way rejoicing." (Acts 8:26–39 NIV, emphasis added)

Nelson's Bible Dictionary gives this definition: "Eunuch [YOO nook]: a male servant of a royal household in Bible times. Such servants were often emasculated by castration as a precautionary measure, especially if they served among the wives in a ruler's harem (2 Kings 9:32)."[1]

So, a eunuch is a man who has been castrated. If altered before adolescence, he lacks the normal testosterone of a male and is usually smaller in frame, with less muscle development and more fat. He does not grow a beard. His voice is higher. He has little or no sex drive. If altered during adulthood, his body frame and lower voice are already established, and the testosterone is then eliminated, decreasing muscle mass and preventing reproduction.

We are shocked. Why would any man be treated this way?

What we are missing is the fact that slavery was the norm of that time. War was the expected way of life. The strong ruled by the sword. The victor killed many people, but he kept some as slaves, and they were treated as less than human. Those he kept were property, *objects to be used.* The eunuch was castrated so he could be used to manage the harem. Some, due to superior intelligence, rose to positions of power under their ruler.

Josephus, a Hebrew historian, reported that the Hebrews did not practice castration of men or animals.

Notice that the eunuch mentioned in this Scripture passage was from Ethiopia, roughly fifteen hundred miles away. He was traveling by chariot. Remember that he did not have our conveniences of auto or air travel. If he averaged thirty miles a day (not likely), it would require fifty days to make the trip. Why and how could anyone afford such travel? He was the treasurer of his nation, and apparently he had gone to the temple in Jerusalem to worship God—probably a once-in-a-lifetime trip. Notice also that he was wealthy enough to have a hand-copied scroll of the Prophets.

To understand the Bible, we must see *conquest, oppression, and slavery as normal for life in that day.* Peace and freedom were dreams, reserved for places like heaven.

Yes. Human life was cheap. It was the ministry of Jesus that gave worth to all life.

CHAPTER 9

WHO CARES ABOUT A LITTLE COIN?

"So, that woman lost a coin somewhere," said Phil. "So what? What good is a single coin anyway?"

"You certainly can't do much with a single coin," Jody answered. "You can't even buy a stick of gum with a penny. I don't know why she was so upset about it."

Let's look first at Jesus' teaching in Luke: "Or suppose a woman has ten silver coins and loses one. Does she not light a lamp, sweep the house and search carefully until she finds it? And when she finds it, she calls her friends and neighbors together and says, 'Rejoice with me; I have found my lost coin.' In the same way, I tell you, there is rejoicing in the presence of the angels of God over one sinner who repents." (Luke 15:8-10 NIV)

In America today, a single coin has little value. But this woman was not in America. She was in Judea or Galilee a long time ago. And this was not any old coin.

Start by remembering that a woman had no worth except her economic value. She had value as a sexual partner. She had value as one who could bear children, preferably males. She had value as one who could collect firewood and water. She had value as one who could prepare meals.

However, she did not own the home where she lived, not even half of it. The culture said that the children were his. She was just the womb that bore them and the breasts that nursed them. She owned *only* the clothing on her back and the few coins that were part of her dowry.

The woman in this passage had lost a coin from her dowry. Such coins had a hole in them and were strung onto strands of animal hide or plant fiber to be worn as ornaments on the forehead, around the neck, or around the wrist. People at that time simply did not have the high-tensile plastic materials available to us, so it is easy to see how the strand holding a coin could have broken and a coin become lost.

But where had she lost it? Was it lost in the house? Was it out in the courtyard? Could she have lost it while getting water or collecting firewood?

The first place to look was in the house. The floors were usually made of stones laid loosely together. There were hundreds of cracks where it could lodge.

And how could she see to find it? The house had little light. If there were any windows, they were small and set high. So she lit a lamp.

What did Jesus mean by "a lamp"? This lamp was a pottery object with a wick sticking out of a narrow neck. It contained olive oil and would make light comparable to a candle.

With that little light and a broom, she began to search.

That missing coin was about 10 percent of all that she owned. *It could never be replaced, because she only got one dowry.* It had come from her family, so it also had sentimental value. Can you see how desperate she was to find it?

Jesus told this story to show how much God values those who are lost from him.

I want you to see the culture Jesus lived in. It will help you understand the Bible if you can begin to understand how little most people had. You may not think of yourself as rich, but compared to an average woman of Judea or Galilee in Jesus' day, most American people are incredibly wealthy. She owned only the few coins of her dowry and the clothing she wore.

When she found her lost coin, it was party time. That is how God feels when a lost soul is found.

CHAPTER 10

WHY BOTHER WITH HER?

"Where do they get words like *Syrophoenician?*" Jody asked.

"I'm not sure I even know how to say that one," Phil replied. "It sure has nothing to do with my town."

Syrophoenician is a word from the New Testament. It refers to a woman that Jesus met. Let's look at the story.

Jesus went away from there, and withdrew into the district of Tyre and Sidon. And a Canaanite woman from that region came out and began to cry out, saying, "Have mercy on me, Lord, Son of David; my daughter is cruelly demon-possessed." But He did not answer her a word. And His disciples came and implored Him, saying, "Send her away, because she keeps shouting at us." But He answered and said, "I was sent only to the lost sheep of the house of Israel." But she came and began to bow down before Him, saying, "Lord, help me!" And He answered and said, "It is not good to take the children's bread and throw it to the dogs." But she said, "Yes, Lord; but even the dogs feed on the crumbs which fall from their masters' table."

Then Jesus said to her, "O woman, your faith is great; it shall be done for you as you wish." And her daughter was healed at once. (Matt. 15:21–28 NASB)

Where exactly does this story take place? The *New Unger's Bible Dictionary* tells us that *Syrophoenician* is "a general name (Mark 7:26) of a female inhabitant of the northern portion of Phoenicia, popularly called Syrophoenicia by reason of its proximity to Syria and its absorption by conquest into that kingdom."[1]

Tyre and Sidon were cities due north of Galilee, on the coast of the Mediterranean Sea. Jesus had to go through Syrophoenicia to get there. He appears to have taken the disciples away from home to get some rest from the crowds.

Why did Jesus talk to her in this condescending way? This sounds like a put-down to us. He was calling her a member of a nation that the Hebrews called dogs—and dogs then were not cuddly house pets. They were wild animals that scavenged for food wherever they could find it. This woman was not a Hebrew, not a member of the house of Israel. In Jewish eyes, she was a dog.

Jesus was drawing out her faith. She knew that she and her people were looked down upon by the Hebrews. Many people would have given up, but she knew that Jesus had the power to heal, and she was desperate for her daughter's sake. She persisted and received her request.

This woman is in many ways like the Samaritan woman discussed in chapter 3. Why would Jesus pay any attention to a woman, let alone this foreign one? To understand the contrast, we must look at the Hebrew attitude toward their own nation.

All Hebrews knew themselves to be "the chosen people of God." Isaiah had prophesied: "I will bring forth descendants from Jacob, and from Judah those who will possess my mountains; *my chosen people* will inherit them, and there will my servants live" (Isa. 65:9 NIV, emphasis added).

There are many variations of this description: *My people, the apple of My eye, children of Abraham*, etc. God had called Abraham (previously called Abram) to obey him by going to a distant country that God would show him. To us, that may not seem important, but this was an *extreme request*. The destination was to be a great distance away. The biggest obstacle was that people then had a permanent attachment to their land. They were never to leave it. They were to live, die, and be buried there. That land was to stay in the family forever. And God's command required Abram to *leave his land and his family*, probably forever.

Abram obeyed God. God made a covenant (a promise, an agreement, a vow) with him. As a result of that relationship, later generations felt that they had a favored position with God. They felt that they had *inherited* the covenant. They felt that God favored them over all the people of the earth. They were his *chosen people*.

However, with this favored position, God had called them to a task: "I, the LORD, have called you in righteousness; I will take hold of your hand. I will keep you and will make you to be a covenant for the people and *a light for the Gentiles*" (Isa. 42:6 NIV, emphasis added).

Somehow the Jews had forgotten the part about being a light. They tried to hold everything for themselves and looked down on all who were not "chosen people."

This explains why Jesus scolded the Pharisees in the gospel of John. "'Abraham is our father,' they [the Pharisees] answered.¶ 'If you were Abraham's children,' said Jesus, 'then you would do the things Abraham did. As it is, you are determined to kill me, a man who has told you the truth that I heard from God. Abraham did not do such things."' (John 8:39–40 NIV).

So the Hebrew people were favored by God *for a relationship and a task*. And God did send his Messiah through them, for they were his chosen people.

Because of this status, Hebrews felt that Samaritans, Phoenicians, Canaanites, and other foreigners were unworthy. Actually, they felt they would be corrupted (made ceremonially unclean) by contact with them.

Notice that Jesus did not share this Hebrew attitude toward other people. He talked to the woman at the well. He healed the daughter of this desperate woman in Syrophoenicia. He healed the servant of the Roman centurion. He came to be the savior of the *world*, not just the Hebrews.

So why bother with her? Because people like her were the lost he came to save.

CHAPTER 11

HOW CAN I TELL THESE GUYS APART?

"I feel like I need a program with descriptions of the cast," Jody complained to Phil. "Who are all these people that Jesus had to deal with constantly?"

To understand the New Testament, we need to understand who the Pharisees were, because they played such a large role.

Nelson's Bible Dictionary defines them this way: "Pharisees [FARE uh sees] (*separated ones*): a religious and political party in Palestine in New Testament times. The Pharisees were known for insisting that the law of God be observed as the scribes interpreted it and for their special commitment to keeping the laws of tithing and ritual purity."[1]

The Pharisees were held in great honor by the people, generally because they were professionals at keeping the law of Moses. This was a full-time job. There were 613 separate laws, more than many people could know and keep. The Pharisees felt they were maintaining God's will by keeping all of these laws. They were rigid and unbending about keeping every detail of the law, as defined by the scribes.

We must also understood a group called the *scribes*. *Nelson's Bible Dictionary* defines them this way: "Scribes: members of a learned class in ancient Israel through New Testament times who studied the Scriptures and served as copyists, editors, and teachers."[2]

Today we would call them lawyers. They were experts in the law of Moses. They were called scribes because originally their primary function was to copy the Scriptures onto new scrolls. Across time, they became the primary interpreters of the law.

These lawyers had to decide issues of the law, such as the commandment not to work on the Sabbath. They were sure of what *Sabbath* meant, but what was considered *work*? William Barclay describes it this way: "For instance, to carry a burden on the Sabbath day is to work. But next a burden has to be defined. So the Scribal Law lays it down that a burden is 'food equal in weight to a dried fig, enough wine for mixing in a goblet, milk enough for one swallow, honey enough to put on a wound, oil enough to anoint a small member, water enough to moisten an eye-salve, paper enough to write a custom's house notice upon, ink to write two letters of the alphabet, reed enough to make a pen—' and so on endlessly."[3]

It was this trivia that Jesus taught against. For example, the scribes felt that healing on the Sabbath was work. "Jesus said to them, 'My Father is always at his work to this very day, and I, too, am working.' For this reason the Jews tried all the harder to kill him; not only was he breaking the Sabbath, but he was even calling God his own Father, making himself equal with God." (John 5:17–18 NIV).

Sadducees is another group frequently mentioned, along with the Pharisees, as opposing Jesus. The *Nelson's Bible Dictionary* defines them as follows: "Sadducees [SAJ uh seez]: members of a Jewish faction that opposed Jesus during His ministry. Known for their denial of the bodily resurrection, the Sadducees came from the leading families of the nation—the priests, merchants, and aristocrats. The high priests and the most powerful members of the priesthood were mainly Sadducees."[4]

Obviously, Jesus got on the wrong side of powerful people. These were the people of wealth who were used to power, used to controlling the events of their nation. It is easy to see why they would not like anyone to rock the boat. They had already made the best of a bad situation. They did not want anyone to upset the delicate balance they had achieved. And it looked as if Jesus was going to try to be the new Messiah, a challenge to Rome's authority.

We often hear of another group as well—the *Levites. Nelson's Bible Dictionary* defines them this way: "Levites [LEE vytes]: descendants of Levi who served as assistants to the *priests* in the worship system of the nation of Israel. As a Levite, Aaron and his sons and their descendants were charged with the responsibility of the priesthood— offering burnt offerings and leading the people in worship and confession. But all the other Levites who were not descended directly from Aaron were to serve as priestly assistants, taking care of the tabernacle and the Temple and performing other menial duties."[5]

These men were descendants of Levi. They were members of one of the twelve tribes of Israel. During the temple periods, as in Jesus' day, these men lived in one of forty-eight cities designated for them. They took their turns serving at the temple, assisting with skinning and preparing the sacrifices, examining lepers, leading music, and so on. Across the years, their dedication to God wavered, just like the rest of the nation.

A strange group that later opposed Jesus was called the *Herodians. Nelson's Bible Dictionary* defines them: "Herodians [heh ROW dih uns]: Jews of influence and standing who were favorable toward Greek customs and Roman law in New Testament times. Although the Herodians should not be equated with the Sadducees, they sided with the Sadducees in their pro-Roman sympathies and opposed the Pharisees, who were anti-Roman. The Herodians joined forces with the Pharisees, however, in their opposition to Jesus."[6]

We can easily see why they would oppose Jesus. They had made peace with their present situation and did not want Jesus to endanger their place in society.

There were many groups in that society, but one more must be mentioned: the *Zealots*. The *Nelson's Bible Dictionary* says, "A Zealot was a member of a fanatical Jewish sect that militantly opposed the Roman domination of Palestine during the first century A.D."[7]

Today we would call them guerilla fighters. They could not stand in ranks against the Roman army, but they could harass them in hit-and-run raids. One of Jesus' disciples was Simon the Zealot. (Can you imagine how he got along with Matthew, a former tax collector and collaborator with Rome?)

Hebrew society was centered on the law of Moses. The Pharisees were the superstars. They tried to keep every letter of the law. The scribes were the interpreters of that law. The Sadducees were the upper crust of the society. The Levites were the temple assistants. The Herodians were the people who sided with King Herod. And the Zealots were those who wanted to break free from Rome by using guerilla warfare, hoping that God would side with them to overthrow their Roman rulers.

The characters in these various groups were not inclined to *real prayer*, or they would have recognized the Messiah when he came. Each faction had its own agenda, and it was not God's.

Let's do a quick summary of this section on cultural problems. The most basic problem, it seems to me, was the poverty of the common people. They lived close to the earth and depended on successful crops and herds to survive. Life was short and hard. When we add male domination of females to the point that they were property, we can see how blighted life was. With the addition of Roman taxation, life became extremely difficult. We can only imagine the weight of oppression that came from the Roman army. They ruled with tyranny and terrorism. Those who survived battles were often made slaves, to be used as we would use animals. Warfare, early death, and slavery were normal.

All of the New Testament must be read and understood in the light of poverty, gender and class oppression, and the terrorism of Rome.

PART III

PROBLEMS UNDERSTANDING HEBREW THEOLOGY

CHAPTER 12

HOW CAN A SAMARITAN BE GOOD?

"It was nice of that Samaritan guy to help," Jody said, "but I don't get all the fuss about it. We're *supposed* to help people."

"Yeah, I know what you mean," Phil agreed.

That is the American view. We do not understand the theological boundaries of the people involved.

First, let's look at the story.

But he wanted to justify himself, so he asked Jesus, "And who is my neighbor?"¶ In reply Jesus said: "A man was going down from Jerusalem to Jericho, when he fell into the hands of robbers. They stripped him of his clothes, beat him and went away, leaving him half dead. A priest happened to be going down the same road, and when he saw the man, he passed by on the other side. So too, a Levite, when he came to the place and saw him, passed by on the other side. But a Samaritan, as he traveled, came where the man was; and when he saw him, he took pity on him. He went to him and bandaged his wounds, pouring on oil and wine. Then he put the man on his own donkey, took him to an inn and took care of him. The next day he took out two silver coins and gave them to the innkeeper. 'Look after him,' he said, 'and when I return, I will reimburse you for any extra expense you may have.'¶ Which of these three do you think was a neighbor to the man who fell into the hands of robbers?"¶ The expert in the law replied, "The one who had mercy on him."¶ Jesus told him, "Go and do likewise." (Luke 10:29–37 NIV)

Now, let's look at the scene of Jesus' story. What they called a road, we would call a footpath today. Do not envision a four-lane highway. It was a path that could be traveled by donkey or on foot. It was cut into the side of a very steep mountain. Travel across it was dangerous, because there were bands of thieves who frequently attacked individuals or small groups of travelers. So the story of an attack here was very realistic.

Now we come to the theological part of the story that we usually miss. The first passerby was a priest. He was on his way home after serving in the temple. He knew the law of Moses. He had to stay *ceremonially clean* to be able to function in the temple. What does that mean? There were many ways to become unclean, but possible contact with this victim was clearly one of them.

"Whoever touches the dead body of anyone will be unclean for seven days. He must purify himself with the water on the third day and on the seventh day; then he will be clean. Whoever touches the dead body of anyone and fails to purify himself defiles the LORD's tabernacle. That person must be cut off from Israel." (Num. 19:11–13a NIV).

The poor man lying on the path might have been dead. The priest felt that he had to stay far away from him, because *his highest duty* was to serve God as a priest in the temple. But he was on his way home *after* serving. He could have allowed himself to become unclean for a week.

But no, being clean was a lifestyle that he chose not to endanger. He stayed far away from this body that might possibly be dead.

Then a Levite saw the victim, and he came to the same conclusion. His highest duty to God was to assist serving in the temple. We can easily see him reasoning that there were many poor and suffering people that surely God knew he would like to help. But someone in his position couldn't risk becoming unclean. He had a higher responsibility.

Then a despised Samaritan came by. He saw a need and responded to it. His help was immediate and prolonged. It cost him time, effort, and money. But he did it.

After telling the story, Jesus asked the lawyer which of the three travelers was a neighbor to the victim. The scribe would not even say the word *Samaritan*. Instead he answered, "The one who had mercy on him."

Jesus' response was that this expert in the law of Moses was to go and *become like a despised Samaritan*. How is that for twisting the dagger?

Here is a lesson for all of us, as Jesus specifically taught on this point. "Then he asked them, 'If one of you has a son or an ox that falls into a well on the Sabbath day, will you not immediately pull him out?'" (Luke 14:5 NIV).

If we are aware of need, we are to do all we can to help.

Can a Samaritan be good? The Hebrews would uniformly say no. Samaritans were half-breeds, idolaters, apostates. It would be impossible for them to be good. But Jesus used Samaritans several times to illustrate goodness.

When the law conflicts with the needs of people, need trumps even the law of Moses.

CHAPTER 13

WHAT DO YOU MEAN BY DEMONS?

"What do you think about demons in the Bible?" questioned Jody.

"Most people think they're just an invention of superstition," Phil answered, "but they are mentioned in the Bible, so I don't know how to think about it."

In America today, many people do not believe in demons. The educational system has relegated demons to the superstitions of a prescientific time. These same people cannot find a spirit in themselves or others. For them, there is no spirit world; there is only matter. Matter is what science engages. There, science functions well. Just look at our technological progress.

I think it is unfortunate—even suicidal—to believe that *only matter matters*. We have been sold a bill of goods. It has been a first-class con job. Our public educational system is solidly under the control of people who use a model for thinking that excludes God. Del Tackett, PhD, author of *The Truth Project*, says clearly, "They will only consider things that are *in* the box."[1] The educational system will only consider things that can be accessed by the scientific method. By excluding everything else, they can honestly say, as does the TV ad: "Science rules."

But an extreme inconsistency is obvious. These same people use the word *angel* routinely. They wear angel jewelry. They send angel greeting cards. They have angel pictures and knickknacks in their homes. It seems they want the good of angels, but they fear the bad of demons. So they tell themselves that demons don't exist. They want the good part of the spirit world, but they deny the bad part.

To hear of the reality of demons, one needs only to talk to missionaries who have served in areas of the world not dominated by the scientific world view.

In Jesus' day, there was no scientific world view. Science had not yet been heard of. Nicolaus Copernicus' work was the starting point of modern science in 1543. William Harvey released his study of the heart as the circulator of blood in 1628. Louis Pasteur confirmed the germ theory in the 1860s.

In Jesus' day, all illness and misfortune were attributed to demon activity. These demons were angel spirits who had sided with Satan when he rebelled against God and had consequently been thrown out of heaven to earth. The Hebrew understanding was that their earthly world was the battleground for spiritual forces, good and evil.

We may better understand the mechanics of disease today. But does anyone want to argue that the underlying cause has changed? Isn't the world today still a battleground between spiritual forces, good and evil?

Let's look at several references to demons in the Bible.

"While they were going out, a man who was demon-possessed and could not talk was brought to Jesus. And when the demon was driven out, the man who had been mute spoke. The crowd was amazed and said, 'Nothing like this has ever been seen in Israel.'" (Matt. 9:32–33 NIV). As a speech/language pathologist today, I would expect that demon possession such as this would be explained as *hysterical conversion*. I have been professionally involved in such a healing. I prayed for direction, and the student's healing was swift and permanent.

A man in the crowd called out, "Teacher, I beg you to look at my son, for he is my only child. A spirit seizes him and he suddenly screams; it throws him into convulsions so that he foams at the mouth. It scarcely ever leaves him and is destroying him. I begged your disciples to drive it out, but they could not." ¶ "O unbelieving and perverse generation," Jesus replied, "how long shall I stay with you and put up with you? Bring your son here."¶ Even while the boy was coming, the demon threw him to the ground in a convulsion. But Jesus rebuked the evil spirit, healed the boy and gave him back to his father. And they were all amazed at the greatness of God. (Luke 9:38–43 NIV)

This situation appears to be an epileptic seizure, now understood to be an electrical storm in the brain. Again, we know some of the causes of epilepsy and have treatments for it. But giving a condition a name and having some treatments for it is not equivalent to controlling or eliminating it.

Let's look at one more example.

They sailed to the region of the Gerasenes, which is across the lake from Galilee. When Jesus stepped ashore, he was met by a demon-possessed man from the town. For a long time this man had not worn clothes or lived in a house, but had lived in the tombs. When he saw Jesus, he cried out and fell at his feet, shouting at the top of his voice, "What do you want with me, Jesus, Son of the Most High God? I beg you, don't torture me!" For Jesus had commanded the evil spirit to come out of the man. Many times it had seized him, and though he was chained hand and foot and kept under guard, he had broken his chains and had been driven by the demon into solitary places. ¶ Jesus asked him, "What is your name?" ¶ "Legion," he replied, because many demons had gone into him. And they begged him repeatedly not to order them to go into the Abyss.¶ A large herd of pigs was feeding there on the hillside. The demons begged Jesus to let them go into them, and he gave them permission. When the demons came out of the man, they went into the pigs, and the herd rushed down the steep bank into the lake and was drowned. ¶ When those tending the pigs saw what had happened, they ran off and reported this in the town and countryside, and the people went out to see what had happened. When they came to Jesus, they found the man from whom the demons had gone out, sitting at Jesus' feet, dressed and in his right mind; and they were afraid. Those who had seen it told the people how the demon-possessed man had been cured. Then all the people of the region of the Gerasenes asked Jesus to leave them, because they were overcome with fear. So he got into the boat and left. (Luke 8:26–37 NIV)

We do not see poor souls like this as part of our lives. Why? Are we are so advanced in science and medicine that we now know that the demon possessed no longer exist? No, they still exist. But our society is shielded from their presence. They live in the hidden wards of our mental institutions and prisons.

Let's not be so in love with science and medicine that we feel that all problems have been solved. Any honest doctor or scientist will tell you that we are only beginning to understand the mysteries of life.

To understand the Bible, we need to know that Hebrew society saw all of life as a battleground between spiritual forces. That principle is still true today.

What do I mean by *demons*? Demons are spiritual beings who oppose God and goodness. They are the opposite of angels. They are all around us. They harass us. They plant doubt everywhere possible. They stir and stoke anger, bitterness, hatred, and jealousy. Your life and mine are battlegrounds between good and evil. God calls you to himself. Satan tries to trip you up and defeat you.

The ultimate battle was fought on Calvary's hill. Satan threw everything he could muster at Jesus. When Jesus died, Satan felt he had won.

But then came Easter morning. *And Jesus was alive.*

CHAPTER 14

WHO ARE YOU MOST AFRAID OF?

"Have you ever seen a leper?" Phil asked. "I wonder what they look like."

"Didn't we see a movie about lepers that some missionary brought?" Jody said. "We don't have lepers here."

But America went into near hysteria in the 1980s. AIDS was sweeping across our nation. People were dying too soon. Near panic set in. What was this unknown killer? At this point in our history, 1.7 million people have been infected. Some 600,000 are currently infected, and new infections occur at the rate of one every 9.5 minutes. Today the panic has subsided. We now feel that AIDS is controllable. But it is still scary.

In Jesus' day, there was a similar panic. It was called *leprosy*. A person with this condition was called a *leper*. *Nelson's Bible Dictionary* defines it this way:

Leprosy: One of the most dreaded diseases of the world, leprosy is caused by a bacillus and is characterized by formation of nodules that spread, causing loss of sensation and deformity. Now treated with sulfone drugs, leprosy is perhaps the least infectious of all known contagious diseases. Hansen's Disease, as it is more properly known, was often misdiagnosed in biblical times. People believed then that it was highly contagious and hereditary. Leviticus 13:1–17 condemned leprosy as a "plague." On the basis of a hair in a scab, a pimple, or a spot on the skin that had turned white, the priest would declare a person to be a leper and would quarantine him for seven days. If no change in the spot occurred by then, the quarantine would be extended another week. At that time, if the spot had started to fade, the leper would be pronounced cured and returned to his normal life. However, if the spot remained or had spread, he was declared unclean and banished. The words scurf and scall are applied to these spots on the skin by various English translations of the Bible (Lev. 13:30).[1]

Notice the word *banished* in the above definition. The people were panicked by this disease. If it did not clear in fourteen days, the leper was banished from the community—out of the house, town, and community. They found company only in the presence of other lepers. They were left to fend for themselves, out there, somewhere. Family could leave food and clothing for them, but they would never again include them in any event.

Why were they so afraid of lepers? They were afraid because the hands and feet of those affected turned white and mysteriously got shorter and shorter. We now know that due to an extreme lack of sensation in the extremities, they had no sense of touch. They did not feel the rats chewing off pieces as they slept. Horrible, isn't it?

Now, let's look at an account of Jesus interacting with the "untouchables" of his day.

As he was going into a village, ten men who had leprosy met him. They stood at a distance and called out in a loud voice, "Jesus, Master, have pity on us!" ¶ When he saw them, he said, "Go, show yourselves to the priests." And as they went, they were cleansed. ¶ One of them, when he saw he was healed, came back, praising God in a loud voice. He threw himself at Jesus' feet and thanked him— and he was a Samaritan. ¶ Jesus asked, "Were not all ten cleansed? Where are the other nine? Has no one returned to give praise to God except this foreigner?" Then he said to him, "Rise and go; your faith has made you well." (Luke 17:12–19 NIV).

Notice that at the beginning of the account, the lepers stood at a distance, as was expected of them. They communicated by yelling. In verse 16, the returning leper saw normal flesh and knew he was healed. He then was not afraid to get close to Jesus. In situations with other lepers, Jesus touched them to heal them.

To understand the Bible, you need to see the extreme fear these conditions caused. This was not a good time to be alive. They had no remedy. There was nowhere to go for help—except to this miracle worker.

Now, add guilt to the isolation these people felt. The leper could not go to the temple, the only place on the face of the earth where they could take a sacrifice for their sins. They could not go to the temple to pray. They could not take their offerings to the temple to give to God. Not only were they isolated from their family and friends, they were totally and permanently walled-off from God by their leprosy.

Can you begin to feel the horror of leprosy this society felt? It was so bad that even Hebrews with leprosy kept company with Samaritans who also had leprosy. They were the untouchables of their day.

CHAPTER 15

IS THERE A LAW AGAINST DOING GOOD?

"You would think those Pharisees would be happy to see a sick person get healed," Jody insisted.

"I don't know why they were such spoilsports," Phil replied.

The Pharisees weren't evil men. They were very sincere men who were doing the best they knew. They were trying with every ounce of their energy to please God. The law of Moses was very clear. They had memorized every word of it. They had spent vast amounts of time trying to understand what that law meant in every imaginable situation of life. They were trying to be perfect students.

Unfortunately, they were human, just like us. Pride has a way of sneaking up on all of us. Self-satisfaction feels very good. That pride can blind us to our own "elephant in the room."

What was their "elephant"? The scribes (lawyers) had taken every one of the 613 laws of Moses and tried to make each one apply to every situation. That way, all one had to do was remember the law of the scribes—and do it. Presto! God would be pleased, and people could say, "I did it all by myself!"

One of those laws of Moses was this:

Remember the Sabbath day by keeping it holy. Six days you shall labor and do all your work, but the seventh day is a Sabbath to the LORD your God. On it you shall not do any work, neither you, nor your son or daughter, nor your manservant or maidservant, nor your animals, nor the alien within your gates. For in six days the LORD made the heavens and the earth, the sea, and all that is in them, but he rested on the seventh day. Therefore the LORD blessed the Sabbath day and made it holy. (Ex. 20:8–11 NIV).

Verse 9 says that no one is to work on the Sabbath day. The Hebrew rulers knew that healing had been defined by the scribes (lawyers) as one form of work, so they were certainly within their rights to complain to Jesus about working on the Sabbath. "Indignant because Jesus had healed on the Sabbath, the synagogue ruler said to the people, 'There are six days for work. So come and be healed on those days, not on the Sabbath.'" (Luke 13:14 NIV).

Before going further, we need to remember that the law of Moses was the center of Hebrew life. It was what boys went to school to learn. It was the code by which life was lived. It was what gave structure to Hebrew society. It was *the* way to please God.

Then Jesus came on the scene. He did miracles, healing and casting out demons. He taught with authority, not as the scribes did when they compared the teaching of one teacher with another. Jesus said, "*I* say to you …" He called himself Son of God and Son of Man. And Jesus healed on the Sabbath.

What is one to make of this conflict? We all know that laws are sometimes waived under particular circumstances. For example, there are speed laws for drivers, but in an emergency, we can be excused for breaking them. Did Jesus' healing have priority over the law that forbade working on the Sabbath? Why?

In absolute terms, Jesus said that the law would never change. "I tell you the truth, until heaven and earth disappear, not the smallest letter, not the least stroke of a pen, will by any means disappear from the Law until everything is accomplished." (Matt. 5:18 NIV). The question becomes, what did Jesus mean by "the Law"? At least three meanings were given to that term: (1) the Ten Commandments, (2) the first five books of our Bible called the Pentateuch, and (3) all of that, plus the interpretations of the scribes.

It is clear that Jesus did *not* include the interpretations of the scribes in his definition of the law. He consistently fought against their interpretations as "laws of man." (This will be developed in the next chapter.)

Though Jesus lived under all of the laws in the Pentateuch, God, in a vision to Peter, revoked all of the dietary laws for Gentiles (anybody who is not a Hebrew). So I find it unlikely that Jesus meant to include them.

It seems to me that Jesus was referring to the Ten Commandments as being unchanged "until everything is accomplished (or fulfilled)." This, it seems to me, refers to the completion of God's plan for the Holy Spirit to guide the lives of his people.

So, what is the priority? Jesus spelled it out very clearly. "Some of the Pharisees asked, 'Why are you doing what is unlawful on the Sabbath?'¶ Jesus answered them, 'Have you never read what David did when he and his companions were hungry? He entered the house of God, and taking the consecrated bread, he ate what is lawful only for priests to eat. And he also gave some to his companions.' Then Jesus said to them, 'The Son of Man is Lord of the Sabbath.'" (Luke 6:2–5 NIV).

Jesus was saying in clear and powerful terms that *he* took priority over the Sabbath. He could do whatever he wanted on the Sabbath, because he was its master. We now know he was saying that he had made the Ten Commandments and that he could—and would— interpret them. He was superior to the scribes (lawyers). It was the Pharisees' task to learn from him.

When need and law came into conflict, Jesus said, need always trumped law. And he had the right to decide the conflict.

CHAPTER 16

IS THE LAW EVER WRONG?

"I just don't understand why Jesus was always fighting with the scribes and Pharisees," Jody said. "It seems like they were always picking at each other."

"Well, they were constantly trying to trap him," Phil said. "That couldn't have been any fun either. They weren't very nice."

No, they weren't very nice. The relationship was tense at best. Later it became publicly antagonistic. They called for Jesus to be killed, done away with. Why?

As explained earlier, the scribes (lawyers) had developed the law of Moses into a massive list of detailed interpretations. They tried to cover every possible application of the 613 laws. All of this had to be memorized, because in that day the average person could not afford a book (scroll). The Pharisees were professionals in trying to know and keep all of these regulations.

William Barclay wrote about the scribal law: "In the middle of the third century A.D. a summary of it was made and codified. That summary was known as the *Mishnah;* it contains sixty-three tractates on various subjects of the Law, and in English makes a book of almost eight hundred pages. Later Jewish scholarship busied itself with making commentaries to explain the *Mishnah.* These commentaries are known as the *Talmud.* Of the Jerusalem *Talmud* there are twelve printed volumes, and of the Babylonian *Talmud* there are sixty printed volumes."[1]

Can you imagine the burden of trying to keep every regulation listed on eight hundred pages, or twelve or sixty volumes? They were really working hard, trying to keep every imaginable application of the law of Moses.

Their intentions were good—at first. But they confused the external keeping of regulations with the internal motive. The law of Moses said in the first commandment that nothing was to come between them and their God. God was to always be first in their lives. But gradually the keeping of regulations replaced love and worship of God. *Their religion came to be all on the outside.*

Jesus railed against this external faith. "Woe to you, teachers of the law and Pharisees, you hypocrites! You are like whitewashed tombs, which look beautiful on the outside but on the inside are full of dead men's bones and everything unclean. In the same way, on the outside you appear to people as righteous but on the inside you are full of hypocrisy and wickedness." (Matt. 23:27–28 NIV).

Their clothing looked good. Their behavior was perfect. Their religious practices were right on target. But their hearts—Jesus said their hearts were filthy. And God looks on the heart.

To illustrate this with another poorly understood practice, let's look at *corban.*

And he said to them: "You have a fine way of setting aside the commands of God in order to observe your own traditions! For Moses said, 'Honor your father and your mother,' and, 'Anyone who curses his father or mother must be put to death.' But you say that if a man says to his father or mother: 'Whatever help you might otherwise have received from me is Corban [that is, a gift devoted to God],' then you no longer let him do anything for his father or mother. Thus you nullify the word of God by your tradition that you have handed down. And you do many things like that." (Mark 7:9–13 NIV).

Nelson's Illustrated Bible Dictionary defines *corban* this way: "Corban [KAWR bahn] (an offering): a word applied to a gift or offering in the Temple which declared that gift dedicated to God in a special sense ... Jesus condemned the Pharisees for encouraging the people to make such gifts to the Temple while neglecting their responsibility to care for their parents (Mark 7:11–13). According to Jesus, this was a clear violation of a higher commandment, 'Honor your father and mother.'"[2]

Jesus was saying that the requirement to honor one's parents included caring for them when they needed help. (We need to remember that there was no Social Security, no assisted-care living, no nursing homes. Elder care was the responsibility of the extended family.) This was in the law of Moses and is one of the Ten Commandments. But the scribes' interpretation of the law violated it by allowing a person to give to the temple what should have been used for their parents' care.

The Ten Commandments are not suggestions; they are commands. But God gave them as broad precepts, not tiny detail. It seems that God's intention was for the devout to follow the leading of his Spirit in deciding the details. The scribes tried to improve on God's plan and created a monster, the scribal law.

The law kills, but the Spirit sets free.

CHAPTER 17

CAN IT BE BAD TO BE GOOD?

"Can you imagine praying out loud on a street corner?" Jody asked.

"Not me," Phil responded. "I sure wouldn't want people to know what I'm praying about."

But the situation was very different in Jesus' day. Being religious was a good thing, and being *really* religious was a way to be admired. "Wow!" a person might say of an outwardly religious person. "Look at him. He knows all of the law of Moses and keeps them so well. Look how long the fringes are on his prayer shawl. He really has it all together. I wish I could be like him." These guys were the superstars of their society.

But Jesus did not agree. "So when you give to the needy, do not announce it with trumpets, as the hypocrites do in the synagogues and on the streets, to be honored by men. I tell you the truth, they have received their reward in full." (Matt. 6:2 NIV).

Hebrews were expected to give to the poor. Almsgiving was the highest act of righteousness. But Jesus stressed the motive for giving. If a person gave in order to draw attention to himself, God did not receive that gift as pure. Human attention was all the reward the giver would receive.

Next Jesus turned to prayer. "And when you pray, do not be like the hypocrites, for they love to pray standing in the synagogues and on the street corners to be seen by men. I tell you the truth, they have received their reward in full." (Matt. 6:5 NIV).

Why would anyone pray on the street corner? There were certain times of the day when one was supposed to pray: 9:00 a.m., noon, and 3:00 p.m. So, if one just happened to be on the street corner when the time arrived, he was bound to pray.

Surely there were many devout Hebrews who prayed with total sincerity. But it was so easy for any ritual to become meaningless. It was so easy for the words to fall empty to the ground. And it was also possible for any person to begin to enjoy the approval of others when he was seen in prayer. "My, what a good person," someone might say of him. "Just look how careful he is to fulfill his prayer duties."

If recognition was a person's motive for praying, God knew it, and human recognition was all the reward that person would receive. It was not a real prayer, and it would not be heard by God.

Then Jesus turned his attention to fasting. "When you fast, do not look somber as the hypocrites do, for they disfigure their faces to show men they are fasting. I tell you the truth, they have received their reward in full." (Matt. 6:16 NIV).

By now we should understand that Jesus was not condemning the acts of giving to the needy, prayer, or fasting. He was saying that we *can* do these things without meaning, that they *can* be totally fake. We *can* be just going through the motions. These things *can* be done so that other people praise us for our good deeds.

Can you see? Jesus was insisting that religion cannot just be something that we put on like clothing. True faith has to start on the inside. Then it makes a difference in the whole person.

External religion is like a mask; it hides what is behind it. Internal faith soaks through the whole being to the surface. It is real.

CHAPTER 18

DID JESUS TEACH
WITHOUT WORDS?

"Why doesn't someone just make a red-letter Bible for us?" Jody said. "That would be so much easier to carry—and remember."

"Boy! That's a good idea," Phil agreed. "Let's talk to the pastor about it."

This idea sounds good on the surface: get rid of the extra stuff and get right down to the core of it—the teachings of Jesus. Why didn't someone think of this before?

Someone did. In fact, a number of people have tried to edit the Bible and put in it only the parts that they felt were important. Most prominent was Thomas Jefferson, who tried—around 1820—to remove all signs of the supernatural from his cut-and-paste edition.

The problem with a red-letter-only edition of the Bible is that it would remove all of the covenant history, all of the prophecy later fulfilled, and all of the foundational material for the New Testament.

But my focus is that it would remove the *actions* of Jesus, *which often spoke more loudly than his words.*

What do I mean? Female oppression was the norm for the period when Jesus lived. He never campaigned against it, never preached against it. But by his actions he demonstrated that females were as capable and worthy as males. He taught Mary in the home of Mary, Martha, and Lazarus. He discussed serious theology with the Samaritan woman at the well. He healed the son of the Syrophoenecian woman. Though only twelve men were named as disciples, there were several women who were closely associated with his followers.

Wars and warriors were as common as flies, until the Romans imposed peace by defeating all opponents and keeping them down with an iron fist. Jesus' one and only teaching against warfare is found in the beatitudes. "Blessed are the peacemakers, for they will be called sons of God" (Matt. 5:9 NIV).

There are numerous teachings, of course, that lead to peaceful attitudes and behaviors.

"You have heard that it was said to the people long ago, 'Do not murder, and anyone who murders will be subject to judgment.' But I tell you that anyone who is angry with his brother will be subject to judgment. Again, anyone who says to his brother, 'Raca,' is answerable to the Sanhedrin. But anyone who says, 'You fool!' will be in danger of the fire of hell." (Matt. 5:21–22 NIV).

"You have heard that it was said, 'Eye for eye, and tooth for tooth.' But I tell you, Do not resist an evil person. If someone strikes you on the right cheek, turn to him the other also. And if someone wants to sue you and take your tunic, let him have your cloak as well. If someone forces you to go one mile, go with him two miles. Give to the one who asks you, and do not turn away from the one who wants to borrow from you." (Matt. 5:38–42 NIV).

These and many other passages do not directly preach against warfare, but they do teach nonresistance and peaceful living.

But Jesus' *life* taught peacemaking. The only time he raised his hand forcefully was in the temple courtyard on behalf of the Gentiles. Their place to pray in the temple had been turned into a marketplace. Jesus was furious that the temple authorities were so unconcerned about the Gentiles that they had deprived them access. Jesus was not angry about some insult to himself. He was angry for the sake of others. Jesus' action was a return to holiness.

The people expected Jesus as the Son of Man to raise an army. Certainly Judas Iscariot expected Jesus to force the Romans out. I think his betrayal was his immature effort to force Jesus' hand, to say, in effect, "Let's get on with the rebellion."

But when betrayed, Jesus went quietly with the temple guard. When he was accused before Herod and Pilate, he did not respond. He acted out his "turn the other cheek" teaching when flogged, taunted, mocked, and finally crucified.

Slavery was as normal as rotten apples. Everywhere the strong ruled by the sword. Those fortunate enough not to be killed were made slaves. At least they were still alive. There was always the chance that they might somehow earn their freedom.

Jesus did not teach against slavery. He had a much larger evil to combat—the sin of humanity. What he did do was to show the worth of a slave by his response to the slave's need. When the centurion came to ask Jesus to heal his servant, Jesus did not respond, "Oh, just go and get another one. Servants are not people. They are just things to be used." That was the common attitude.

When Jesus had entered Capernaum, a centurion came to him, asking for help. "Lord," he said, "my servant lies at home paralyzed and in terrible suffering."¶ Jesus said to him, "I will go and heal him." (Matt. 8:5–7 NIV).

My point is that Jesus taught powerfully by his actions. We tend to think of teaching as being done by words, spoken or written. But Jesus was a hands-on teacher. He used words *and actions.*

Unless we understand the theological boundaries of these people, we will often misunderstand a passage. All of life was seen as a battle between God and Satan. Good was a blessing from God; bad was from Satan or his demons. For the Hebrews, the law of Moses was the settled truth about God. Nothing in life could be as important. They felt that the first five books of the Bible spelled out these laws. To be sure, the scribes interpreted them in numbing detail. The laws of the scribes meant that no work could be done on the Sabbath, including healing. Those laws covered even what could be eaten and which people you could associate with.

To understand the Bible, we must see the place the Hebrews gave to the law of Moses. It was their code for living. But eventually the code became more important to them than the God who had given it.

Part IV

Problems with the Hebrew Language

CHAPTER 19

WHY IS THEIR WRITING SO SPARSE?

"I don't know why, but the language of the Bible seems funny to me," Jody complained.

"It sure is different from the way we talk," Phil responded.

Yes. It is different. Our writers are much more descriptive than those of the Bible. Look at this sample.

His conniving wife, Judith, came breezily into the sitting room and accusingly asked him, "Why are you so upset that you refuse to eat the delicious food set before you?" ¶ Arnold answered sullenly, "I talked to Nathan Dimner, the antique repairman from J. Jonathan's. I politely said to him, 'Sell me your Waterford vase, or if you prefer, I will give you another vase of greater value for it.' But Nathan immediately snarled and refused." ¶ Judith answered with a sneer, "Is this how you rule as king over the pawn shop? Get right up, eat something with chocolate in it, and cheer up. I will get Nathan's Waterford vase for you."

Have you ever read that before? It's not likely, because I just wrote it. I added a lot of descriptive words to a Bible passage and changed the proper nouns so you wouldn't immediately recognize it. It sounds a lot like our writing of today. I wanted to make the point that the writing of the Bible is very sparse. The writers of the Bible had to be very economical, because writing at that time was so wildly expensive.

For us, print is cheap. But it wasn't that way before Johannes Gutenberg invented the printing press in 1455. Before that, every page had to be written or copied by hand, one letter at a time. The labor costs were extreme.

We think nothing of throwing away a piece of paper. It is just garbage. But the writing surface for the Bible was very expensive. It was parchment made from an animal skin by tanning, or papyrus made from interwoven reeds that were pounded together. (Notes were made on broken pieces of pottery, called shards or potsherds. There were no sticky notes.) So, writing surfaces for a Bible were available only to the wealthy.

Ink was not cheap either. It had to be handmade from charcoal or rare dyes. (Of course, the common person simply picked up a partly burned stick and wrote with it on a broken piece of pottery.)

Therefore, the amount of writing found in a Bible was not available to the common person. The only individuals who could afford to have a copy of a Bible were kings or merchant princes.

Because of this extreme expense, the writers were very economical with their words. They only wrote what was necessary to carry along the meaning of their story.

Now, I want to illustrate this economy by going back to what I wrote at the beginning of the chapter. First, let me show you the words I added or changed. They are in italics.

His *conniving* wife, *Judith*, came *breezily* into the *sitting room* and *accusingly* asked him, "Why are you so upset that you refuse to eat the *delicious food set before you*?" ¶ *Arnold* answered *sullenly*, "I talked to *Nathan Dimner*, the *antique repairman* from *J. Jonathan's*. I *politely* said to him, 'Sell me your *Waterford vase*, or if you prefer, I will give you another *vase of greater value* for it.' But *Nathan immediately snarled* and refused." ¶ *Judith* answered *with a sneer*, "Is this how you rule as king over the *pawn shop*? Get *right* up, eat something *with chocolate in it*, and cheer up. I will get *Nathan's Waterford vase* for you."

The word *conniving* is not used in any translations that I checked. Neither is *sullenly* or *chocolate* or words like them. These words that we use so readily to describe our word pictures simply were not used in writing at that time.

There are just seventy-four words in the original Scripture passage below. There are 111 words in my corruption of the original. That is a 47 percent increase in the number of words. Now, read 1 Kings 21:5–7 (NCV) to see how the verses appeared before I added the descriptive words.

His wife, Jezebel, came in and asked him, "Why are you so upset that you refuse to eat?" ¶ Ahab answered, "I talked to Naboth, the man from Jezreel. I said, 'Sell me your vineyard, or if you prefer, I will give you another vineyard for it.' But Naboth refused."¶ Jezebel answered, "Is this how you rule as king over Israel? Get up, eat something, and cheer up. I will get Naboth's vineyard for you." (1 Kings 21:5-7 NCV)

Can you see how sparse the wording is, how economical the writer was in his use of words? Writers of Scripture used just enough words to carry along their story line or to paint their word pictures.

What does this mean to us? We can be quite sure that there were many more details available at the time of the event. We cannot be absolutely sure what those details were. Arguing with others about what "might have been" is not profitable. We can add details that are reasonable and likely, as long as we do not do violence to what is there. Most preachers do this routinely.

A person of few words can be misunderstood. A torrent of words is likely ignored. What we want is what the little bear in the folk tale wanted: enough to get it "just right."

CHAPTER 20

WHAT WAS OMITTED OR CHANGED?

Jody pointed to a bumper sticker. "What in the world does 'ILVU' mean?" she asked.

"That one is easy," said Phil. "It says, 'I love you.' The I stands for I—"

"Okay, I get it," Jody responded with a smirk. "You don't have to spell it out."

We feel totally comfortable omitting things that we are sure will be understood. Look at all the things that are abbreviated, especially since texting has arrived. That works in our culture, but can you imagine the confusion for someone from another time or place looking at "ILVU"?

Let me give you another example. You know what is meant by, "Hello, beauti—" It would not be "beauti*some*" or "beauti*whole*" or "beauti*able*." It has to be "beauti*ful*." That is the one ending we are used to. It is part of our language, part of our culture.

That is exactly the same mental process that allowed the Bible writers to say themselves, "I don't have to put in that word. Everyone will know what I mean if I leave it out. We have to keep costs down and keep the materials from getting too bulky and heavy to carry."

It was exactly this process that allowed the Hebrews to omit the vowels in all writing. They left out the vowels in the name *Yhwh* (or *Yahweh*, which means "Jehovah" to us). They all knew what the missing vowels were. But since that time, many of us are no longer certain. We think God's name was spelled *Yahweh*, but we can't be sure.

Differences are not always omissions. Sometimes other changes are made. Let's compare two translations of a passage from the Bible. I want to use *Young's Literal Translation*, which is word-for-word, and compare it to *The Message*, which is a paraphrase. (A paraphrase does not translate word-for-word but tries to put the whole idea into our pattern of speaking and writing.)

And at midnight Paul and Silas praying, were singing hymns to God, and the prisoners were hearing them, and suddenly a great earthquake came, so that the foundations of the prison were shaken, opened also presently were all the doors, and of all—the bands were loosed; and the jailor having come out of sleep, and having seen the doors of the prison open, having drawn a sword, was about to kill himself, supposing the prisoners to be fled, and Paul cried out with a loud voice, saying, "Thou mayest not do thyself any harm, for we are all here." (Acts 16:25–28 YLT)

Now, compare that to *The Message*.

Along about midnight, Paul and Silas were at prayer and singing a robust hymn to God. The other prisoners couldn't believe their ears. Then, without warning, a huge earthquake! The jailhouse tottered, every door flew open, all the prisoners were loose.¶ Startled from sleep, the jailer saw all the doors swinging loose on their hinges. Assuming that all the prisoners had escaped, he pulled out his sword and was about to do himself in, figuring he was as good as dead anyway, when Paul stopped him: "Don't do that! We're all still here! Nobody's run away!" (Acts 16:25–28 MSG)

The first translation has 103 words; the second has one hundred. So in this case, length is not the issue. Let's compare phrases first.

> "And at midnight" becomes "along about midnight."
> "Singing hymns to God" becomes "singing a robust hymn to God."
> "The prisoners were hearing them" becomes "the other prisoners couldn't believe their ears."
> "And suddenly a great earthquake came" becomes "then, without warning, a huge earthquake."
> "So that the foundations of the prison were shaken" becomes "the jailhouse tottered."
> "Opened presently were all the doors" becomes "every door flew open."
> "And of all—the bands were loosed" becomes "all the prisoners were loose."

What was omitted? Nothing. We understand all the words of *Young's Literal Translation*. The problem is that the phrasing is not done the way we presently think or talk. *The Message* does not omit letters to form abbreviations. It does not omit words, because the word count is almost the same. What is different is this: the construction of the phrases seems so much more comfortable for us in *The Message*.

It is a matter of opinion. Should the Bible be presented in a "holy language" or in a language we understand easily? Which do you prefer?

CHAPTER 21

ARE THESE THINGS IN ORDER OR NOT?

"I don't know why they don't get everything in order," complained Jody. "It mixes me up."

"Yeah, I know what you mean," agreed Phil. "It is confusing."

It doesn't make sense to us, but the people of Bible times did not use the exact sequencing that we expect. Let's look first at genealogy. The lists in Matthew and Luke are not exactly alike. The *IVP Bible Background Commentary* says, "Matthew omits some names, as was customary in genealogies (in this case perhaps following the Greek translation of the Old Testament); creating patterns like three sets of fourteen made lists easier to remember."[1]

We need to remember that Scripture was written before printing was available. Everything had to be held in the memory of the community. So all materials were presented in a way that made them easier to recall. These patterns of fourteen were a memory aid.

Let's look again at the *IVP Bible Background Commentary.* "Like Greco-Roman genealogies, but unlike Matthew and Old Testament genealogies, Luke starts with the most recent names and works backward. This procedure enables him to end with 'Son of God'. Scholars have proposed various explanations for the differences between the genealogies of Matthew and Luke, of which the following are most prominent: (1) one (probably Matthew) records the genealogy of Joseph, the other of Mary; (2) one (probably Matthew) spiritualizes the genealogy rather than following it literally; (3) the lines of descent cross but are different because one list includes several adoptive lines through levirate marriages (Deut. 25:5–10)."[2]

Our ancestry searches would be very difficult if we did it that way.

Another problem is caused by technology differences. We wear wristwatches and use day planners, smartphones, etc., to plan our day.

Their situation was extremely different from ours. Our technology was not available to them. They told time by units of the day called *watches.* This was the amount of time spent in the tower, *watching* for potential invading armies. The Hebrews measured days by sunrise and sunset. They measured years by the seasons. They did not have the moment-by-moment requirements that we do to accurately use or report time. In that culture, you would never hear someone say, "He died at 10:47 a.m." If they reported a time at all, it would be, "He died in the second watch."

People in our workforce live under the tyranny of time, achieving more productivity in less time. It is called *efficiency.* The Hebrews lived under the tyranny of warfare, a short lifespan, and a scarce food supply.

The *Dictionary of Biblical Imagery* says, "The ancients, who had neither wristwatches nor appointment books and did not live with technology's demand for exact numbers, did not in general share our preoccupation with numerical or chronological precision."[3]

Due to changes in technology, people of the Bible were not as concerned as we are with accuracy in reporting time. They accurately reported the way things were. We have no right to try to impose our standards on them.

CHAPTER 22

DON'T THESE WORDS MEAN WHAT THEY SAY?

"I just don't understand why a word in the Bible doesn't mean what it says," charged Jody.

"I agree," said Phil. "A word should mean what it says. It doesn't make sense to me either."

As Gertrude Stein famously wrote in 1935, "A rose is a rose is a rose is a rose." True. But a word is not always a word. It does not always mean what it seems to mean. For example, the word *believe* has a much more precise meaning for us than it did for Jesus and his people. To us, *believe* refers to a mental position we hold. If we say, "I really do *believe* there are aliens," our minds are making that choice.

To the Hebrews, believing meant to throw one's whole life into that position. They would be amazed that we separate our being into body, mind, and spirit. For them, believing meant that they would carry out every bit of their belief. Otherwise, they were lying.

Now we can understand Jesus' words: "The work of God is this: to believe in the one he has sent." (John 6:29b NIV). For Jesus, *believe* meant to give one's entire life to him.

Bowels makes us think of digestion and possibly intestinal gas and elimination. But to the Hebrews, it referred to their inner being. They used *bowels* much as we use the word *heart*. It is usually translated "heart" in modern translations.

We expect the word *disciple* to describe a student who wants to learn from the master. To us it is an intellectual exercise. To the Hebrews it meant learning the *whole life*. They not only wanted to learn the knowledge and wisdom of the teacher, but they also wanted to learn to *live* like him. A disciple or student of Sigmund Freud might later take further that field of study. The only instances where Jesus' disciples took the Christian faith "further" were geographical and technological in nature. They followed his command to "go into all the world," but they never surpassed Jesus in teaching or life.

About the word *forever*, James M. Efird wrote, "The Hebrew mind-set did not really have a concept of forever in the Greek mode; when the Hebrews used the word translated 'forever' (literally it means 'to the age'), this usually carried the connotation of either a long undefined period of time or a unit of time that had a specific or definite conclusion."[1]

However, *Vine's Expository Dictionary of Biblical Words* says, "In other places (Isa. 26:4) the word means 'without beginning, without end, and ever-continuing': 'Trust ye in the lord forever; for in the Lord Jehovah is everlasting strength.'"[2]

It seems the experts do not agree. Who is right? Take your pick!

We expect that the word *heart* refers to the organ that pumps blood, or to the seat of emotions. The Hebrews knew nothing about the heart pumping blood. It wasn't until 1628, when William Harvey published his research, that the heart's function was understood. *Heart* to the Hebrews meant the entire inner person, the core of a person, and it included the mind, will, emotion, character, and many other words we associate with our *whole inner being.*

Our common understanding of the *law of Moses* would be the Ten Commandments. To the Hebrew, that *could* be correct. But it could also refer to the first five books of our Bible, called the Pentateuch. In some cases it referred to the scribes' interpretation of the law, or even to the entire Old Testament. They knew by the context which meaning was correct.

We expect a *master* to be an expert in his or her field, an instructor or a professor. To the Hebrew, the *master* or *rabbi* was the unquestioned authority of his group, who taught intellectual content *and life.* When Peter challenged Jesus' intention to go to Jerusalem, he severely violated the cultural norm. We often see Scripture that says, "They did not dare ask him any more!"

We think of a *meek* person as someone who is easily walked-over—a shy, fearful individual. In the Bible, *meek* refers to a person's conscious choice to restrain his strength or power, because he realizes that God is ultimately in control.

We expect *mercy* to mean pardon or forgiveness for a wrong we have done. To the Hebrews, it meant understanding a person *in depth* by having "walked in their shoes."

We define *knowledge* as accumulated facts and figures in the brain. To the Hebrews, *knowledge* meant having experienced something intimately.

To us, *peace* means the end of conflict. The Hebrew word for *peace* was *shalom*, and it was used to say both "hello" and "good bye."

But *shalom* did not refer to the cessation of conflict. It referred to a state of peace, a prosperous relationship between two or more parties, or feeling at ease or comfortable with someone. It spoke of completeness, where a relationship was one of harmony and wholeness, and of one's welfare and health.

To us, *perfect* refers to total purity or a complete lack of flaws. To the Hebrew it meant *maturity*, becoming all that God created one to be. Carried with this meaning is the concept of "blooming where you are planted," not trying to be more than one is, but fulfilling *totally* God's call on one's life. Now we can understand Jesus words: "Be perfect, therefore, as your heavenly Father is perfect." (Matt. 5:48 NIV). He was telling us to become all that God created us to be.

To us, *prophecy* means seeing into the future, and the prophets did indeed foretell Jesus' coming. But to the Hebrew, *prophecy* meant "speaking the message" from God. Usually that message was a warning to God's people to return to him or face judgment. A small percentage of the "messages from God" did look into the future.

Since these word meanings in Scripture are so different from what we expect, we need to *deliberately look for the Hebrew meaning*. What looks like a contradiction will disappear when we think the Hebrew way.

Words shift their meanings constantly in a living language, a language spoken by the common people. We should not be so sure that we always know what someone else means!

CHAPTER 23

WHAT DOES THIS SYMBOL MEAN?

"Boy! Talk about being confused!" Phil grumbled. "I would never have figured out what that symbol on the cross meant."

"I agree," Jody replied. "That one was way beyond me."

Jody and Phil were referring to the "IHS" on the cross that was on the altar at their church. It is a symbol that completely eludes most American worshippers. It stands for "JESUS."

How in the world do they get that?

The abbreviation style of earlier days was different from ours. In abbreviations, we use the first letter of each word, but they used the first *several* letters. So they used "JES" for "JESUS." The letters do not look right to us because they are Greek. Their "J" looks like an "I" to us, and their "E" looks like an "H." It is a problem of abbreviating style and understanding another language.

To understand the Bible, we have to deal with symbols, which were a large part of Hebrew culture. The *Dictionary of Biblical Imagery* says, "A symbol is an image that stands for something in addition to its literal meaning. It is more laden with meaning than the connotations of the straight image. In the overwhelming majority of cases, symbolism emerges as a shared language in a culture."[1]

To our Western eyes, many biblical symbols are strange or curious. They are not easily understood by readers from our culture. The Hebrews' symbols were as well understood to them as our figures of speech are to us.

The following list was started from *The Comprehensive Analysis of the Bible*, written by Montgomery F. Essig.[2] I have selected from it only those symbols that are *consistent across three major translations*: the *King James Version* (the favorite of our childhood), the *New American Standard Bible* (a very accurate word-for-word translation), and the *New International Version* (the most popular contemporary translation). Note that the symbolic *word* is not always used as a symbol. It is often used literally as well as symbolically—and sometimes in secondary forms such as a verb or an adjective.

Symbol	Meaning	References
adultery	idolatry	Jer. 3:8–9; 5:7; Rev. 2:22
angel	messenger or minister	Rev. 2:1
arm	power or strength	Ps. 10:15; Ezek. 30:21
arrows	judgment	Deut. 32:23; Job 6:4
Babylon	city of evil	Rev. 16:19
beast	tyrant	Daniel 7:17; Rev. 18:4
blindness	ignorance	Isa. 29:1
bride	church of Christ	Rev. 21:9
bridegroom	Christ married to his church	John 3:29

candlesticks/ lampstands	churches	Rev. 1:12
crown	victory or reward	James 1:12; Rev. 2:10
day	indefinite period	Isa. 34:8; Rev. 2:10
dogs	impure people	Ps. 22:16; Matt. 15:26
dragon	Satan	Rev. 12:9; 20:2
eyes	knowledge	Prov. 15:3
face	fellowship with God	Ps. 27:8
fat	abundance	Jer. 5:28
fire	judgment	Isa. 42:25
forehead	public profession	Ezek. 9:4; Rev. 7:3
furnace	affliction	Jer. 11:4
garments, clothes	outward appearance	Isa. 61:10; Rev. 3:4
gates	strength, security	Ps. 147:13
goats	wicked people	Matt. 25:33
grass	lower order of plants	Rev. 8:7; 9:4
hail	divine vengeance	Isa. 30:30; Rev. 11:19
hand of the Lord	divine influence	Ezek. 8:1
harvest	time of destruction	Joel 3:13
heavens	political governments	Hag. 2:21
hunger and thirst	spiritual desire	Matt. 5:6
incense	prayer	Rev. 5:8
keys	power, authority	Rev. 1:18
lamp	successor, descendent	1 Kings 15:4; Ps. 132:17
light	joy, prosperity	Est. 8:16; Matt. 11:29–30
mountains	a state, a country	Zech. 4:7; Isa. 2:2
mystery	now understood	Rom. 16:25
naked	in sinful state	Rev. 3:17

night	adversity, ignorance	Isa. 21:12; Rev. 21:25
oaks	men of rank, power	Isa. 2:13
oil	abundance, joy	Ps. 23:5; 92:10
paradise	heaven	Luke 23:43; Rev. 2:7
right hand	protection or support equal authority	Ps. 18:35; 73:23, Matt. 26:64
rock	a secure refuge	Ps. 18:2
salt	purity or barrenness	Ps. 2:9; Deut. 29:23
serpent	the Devil	Gen. 3:1–2; 2 Cor. 11:3
sheep	Christ's disciples	John 10:11, 16
shepherds	rulers, civil or church	Nah. 3:18; Ezek. 34:2
shield	defense or protection	Ps. 84:9; Eph. 6:16
sleep	death	1 Thess. 4:14
star	prince or ruler	Nah. 24:17
sword	war, slaughter	Isa. 34:5; Ezek. 21:3
vine	people of Israel	Ps. 80:8
vineyard	people of Israel	Isa. 5:1
watchman	prophet	Ezek. 3:17
wings	protection	Ps. 17:8
woman	a city or state	Rev. 12:1
yoke	labor or restraint	Deut. 28:48

Symbols often allowed the Hebrew concrete thinkers to express abstract thoughts. Certainly they were also used at times to hide the meaning from the eyes of outsiders.

To understand the Bible, we need to be able to interpret the symbols the writers used.

CHAPTER 24

CAN THIS MEAN WHAT IT SOUNDS LIKE?

"Did you make any sense of that 'coals of fire on their head' thing in the Scripture lesson?" asked Jody.

"It sounds like *torture* to me," offered Phil.

Figures of speech cause a lot of problems for us.

As a speech/language pathologist working in the public schools, I was tasked with helping two sisters, aged seven and nine, to learn to speak our language. They had come to America from India without knowing a word of English. Teaching them the names of real objects was not difficult, and they quickly caught on to actions. But the *idioms* their peers used completely baffled them.

Why don't people say what they mean? "I've got a frog in my throat." "You're pulling my leg!" "It's raining cats and dogs!" Why don't people talk so they can be understood?

Babies learn language from the people around them, and strange as it may seem, people who live with sayings like these understand them. Their culture regularly uses these figures of speech, so the sayings are absorbed without thinking about how odd they may sound to a stranger. Native speakers understand them and use them easily. They are called *idioms*. An idiom does not mean literally what it says. "Oh, Mom will just kill me!" doesn't mean that at all.

Interestingly, it seems that all languages use idioms. They are even found in the Bible. So, when our Bible translators are very accurate in word-for-word translation, we are just as puzzled as Jody was. We don't understand the idiom either! Obviously, as children we were never exposed to Bible idioms in our day-to-day language.

The following Old Testament idioms are found in the material by Wayne Lehman at his website.[1]

What in the world did the Hebrew writer mean by *sweet water*? Was it water with sugar or honey added? "Then Moses cried out to the LORD, and the LORD showed him a piece of wood. He threw it into the water, and the *water became sweet*." (Ex. 15:25a NIV, emphasis added). In this case, *sweet* means "fit to drink."

The *New Living Translation* and the *New English Translation* have translated the idiom correctly. "So Moses cried out to the LORD for help, and the LORD showed him a piece of wood. Moses threw it into the water, and this made the *water good to drink*." (Ex. 15:25a NLT).

"Their throat is an open grave" sounds like someone is buried in another person's throat. "Not a word from their mouth can be trusted; their heart is filled with destruction. *Their throat is an open grave*; with their tongue they speak deceit." (Ps. 5:9 NIV).

Again, the *New Living Translation* has it right. "My enemies cannot speak a truthful word. Their deepest desire is to destroy others.

Their talk is foul, like the stench from an open grave." (Ps. 5:9 NLT). "Throat is an open grave" means that their speech is rotten, foul, and evil.

What does "breaking the yoke" mean to a society that barely knows what a yoke is? "'So I will go to the leaders and speak to them; surely they know the way of the LORD, the requirements of their God.' But with one accord they too had *broken off the yoke* and *torn off the bonds*." (Jer. 5:5 NIV).

This time the best translation is in the *New English Translation*. "To break the yoke" means "to reject authority." Notice also that "torn off the bonds" is another idiom meaning "refusing to submit." "'I will go to the leaders and speak with them. Surely they know what the LORD demands. Surely they know what their God requires of them.' Yet all of them, too, have *rejected his authority* and *refuse to submit to him*." (Jer. 5:5 NET).

The New Testament idioms are no less strange to us. A most perplexing idiom is found in the gospel of John. "Whoever *eats my flesh and drinks my blood* has eternal life, and I will raise him up at the last day." (John 6:54 NIV). This certainly sounds like cannibalism! The early church was even accused of it because of misunderstanding about Holy Communion.

In *Bible Idioms: Did You Mean What I Think You Said?*,[2] Dave Miller interprets this to mean "to consume His words and live by them." This is supported a few verses later, where Jesus said, "The words I have spoken to you are spirit and they are life." (John 6:63b NIV).

However, *IVP Bible Background Commentary* comments, "Jesus provides here the interpretive key to what preceded: he is not speaking literally, as if they are to eat his literal flesh; he speaks of his gift of the Spirit" (John 6:63).[3]

Further, *The Bible Exposition Commentary* states: "Second, He made it clear that He was not speaking in literal terms (John 6:63). He was using a human analogy to convey a spiritual truth, just as He did with Nicodemus and the Samaritan woman."[4]

These three agree that the meaning is not literal, but they differ slightly on how to correctly translate the idiom. We can see here the difficulty that translators have with some idioms they have not grown up with.

Another idiom with serious results is this: "And if your eye causes you to sin, *gouge it out and throw it away.*" (Matt. 18:9a NIV). It has been reported that some followers took this idiom literally and blinded themselves.

I have twenty-four other translations on my computer, and all translate this as self-mutilation. However, George Lamsa says that it means, "Stop it, cut it out!"[5] Since this is an idiom, I believe Lamsa is correct.

Many are confused by this statement of Jesus: "For as Jonah was three days and three nights in the belly of a huge fish, so the Son of Man will be *three days and three nights* in the heart of the earth." (Matt. 12:40 NIV). We naturally understand this statement from our Greek point of view. To us it means all day Friday, all day Saturday, and all day Sunday. That is three days, and in our culture, each day starts at midnight!

Then we turn to the crucifixion account and see Jesus dying on Friday afternoon, being in the grave all day Saturday, and rising on Sunday morning. From our point of view, that is just a bit over one day! But Scripture clearly says "days and nights."

What we do not understand is the Hebrew way of counting days. E. W. Bullinger says, "The fact is that the *idiom* covers any part of 'three days and three nights.'"[6]

So, from the Hebrew point of view, Jesus' burial began on Friday before sundown (and therefore includes the whole day of Friday). He remained buried on Saturday and rose from dead during Sunday, which began at the prior sundown (again including the whole day), which equals three days. This is an idiom. It cannot be interpreted literally!

Another troublesome idiom is Jesus' fasting in the desert for "forty days and forty nights." By our way of thinking, Jesus should have died from fasting that long. Let's look at the ways that idiom is used, because it is found throughout the Bible.

The flood fell on the earth to destroy evil. Noah and his family survived in the ark. "And rain fell on the earth *forty days and forty nights.*" (Gen. 7:12 NIV).

Moses met with God to receive the laws of God. "Then Moses entered the cloud as he went on up the mountain. And he stayed on the mountain *forty days and forty nights.*" (Ex. 24:18 NIV).

Moses returned to the mountain to receive the Ten Commandments. "Moses was there with the LORD *forty days and forty nights* without eating bread or drinking water. And he wrote on the tablets the words of the covenant—the Ten Commandments." (Ex. 34:28 NIV).

Elijah fled from Jezebel's wrath. "So he got up and ate and drank. Strengthened by that food, he traveled *forty days and forty nights* until he reached Horeb, the mountain of God." (1 Kings 19:8 NIV).

Jesus was tempted in the wilderness. "After fasting *forty days and forty nights*, he [Jesus] was hungry." (Matt. 4:2 NIV).

The *Dictionary of Biblical Imagery* explains: "Forty is usually just a round number or estimation, not a precise reckoning. The ancients, who had neither wristwatches nor appointment books and did not live with technology's demand for exact numbers, did not in general share our preoccupation with numerical nor chronological precision ... In accord with this sort of imprecision, forty days means a relatively long time."[7]

Idioms can be obvious—or very confusing. Many are well translated by the most recent translations. Some meanings are not translated for fear of being wrong, and some are translated word-for-word. But beware: idioms can be "clear as mud"! Do not build or accept teachings that take as literal words that were always used as an idiom, a figure of speech.

This section on language presents serious problems that we encounter in trying to understand the Bible. We find our own way of reading or writing very natural, and we expect it from others. But living language changes constantly, including the meanings of words. Due to the cost of writing, the Bible writers were very economical with their words. We expect much more detail and feel cheated by its absence. We expect all sequenced material to be in precise order. The Hebrew writers did not worry about skipping things they expected to be understood. Their symbols and idioms can be absolutely frustrating to us.

No, even good translation is just the first step in understanding the Bible.

PART V

PROBLEMS UNDERSTANDING HEBREW THINKING

CHAPTER 25

HOW CAN I DEAL WITH THEIR PICTURES?

"Can you make any sense of Revelation?" Jody asked. "Or Ezekiel? Or Daniel? Animals with four heads, and stuff like that?"

"Not really," Phil responded. "I think it's all very confusing."

Jody and Phil have a lot of company. The word pictures of the Hebrews are very foreign to us. *We just do not think that way.*

The Hebrews knew how to paint pictures with words. Long before cameras existed, they were able to describe real events and even explain emotional states. They did this with word pictures.

We are so used to Greek logic that we incorrectly presume that all thinking has always been logical. What many have not considered is that logic was not developed until after all of the Old Testament was written. Logic did not even affect all of the New Testament. Since they did not have logic available to use, the Hebrews developed word pictures to a high level.

One of our biggest problems in understanding the Bible is a result of the form the material takes. *Logic is not the best tool for understanding Hebrew word pictures.* Actually, logic sometimes leads us astray.

Hebrew word pictures are stories, parables, or comparisons. Each of these forms is rich in meaning, allowing a central point and many secondary points. One example is found in Luke 18:9–14 in the parable of the Pharisee and the tax collector.

To some who were confident of their own righteousness and looked down on everybody else, Jesus told this parable: "Two men went up to the temple to pray, one a Pharisee and the other a tax collector. The Pharisee stood up and prayed about himself: 'God, I thank you that I am not like other men—robbers, evildoers, adulterers—or even like this tax collector. I fast twice a week and give a tenth of all I get.' "But the tax collector stood at a distance. He would not even look up to heaven, but beat his breast and said, 'God, have mercy on me, a sinner.' "I tell you that this man, rather than the other, went home justified before God. For everyone who exalts himself will be humbled, and he who humbles himself will be exalted." (Luke 18:9–14 NIV).

The *central* point is this: a right relationship with God is a gift from God and cannot be earned. Secondary points are: (1) God's gift cannot be received by one who is arrogant, judgmental, and self-satisfied; (2) informing God of one's virtues is not prayer; a real hunger for God's grace is the starting point of real prayer; (3) self-righteousness distorts our view of the world and of God; (4) only those who sense their unworthiness in the presence of God can really receive from him, and (5) rituals are not pleasing to God unless they are accompanied by listening to God and obeying him. (The above paragraph is a paraphrase of material brilliantly discussed in Kenneth Bailey's *Jesus through Middle Eastern Eyes*.)

If a Greek/Westerner were to reduce that parable to an abstract statement, such as, "We can only approach God in humility," we would miss all of the secondary points. Our abstract statement is easy and comfortable for us, but it could also lose a whole lot of the meaning!

The following passage from Psalm 91 draws several pictures. First we find a picture of God as a place of safety, a fort (verse 2), then a picture of God as a protector, a savior (verse 3), then as a hen, and finally as a soldier's shield and protective hill (verse 4).

I will say of the LORD, "He is my refuge and my fortress, my God, in whom I trust [safety]."¶ Surely he will save you from the fowler's snare and from the deadly pestilence [protector].¶ He will cover you with his feathers, and *under his wings* you will find refuge [savior]; his faithfulness will be your shield and rampart. (Ps. 91:2–4 NIV, emphasis added).

Unfortunately for us, these pictures can lead to misunderstanding. For example, God does not have wings, yet the passage *is* talking about God. He is named in verse two, and verse four says, "under his wings."

This is not just a Hebrew problem but a human one. How can we think about or talk about something for which we have no words? The answer is that we make *comparisons* to things that we do understand and have words for.

When I was a boy, most people I knew kept chickens. Our family had a chicken coop and a chicken yard. We understood well the behavior of chickens because we saw it every day. All of us had seen a mother hen call her chicks to her at the first sign of danger, and pull them close to her feet with her wings. The chicks were hidden and sheltered from danger by the wings of the mother hen.

So, the psalm writer used a clearly understood part of everyday life to make a comparison. Just as a mother hen protects her chicks, God will provide cover and protection for those who rely on him.

There was no intent to describe what God *looks like*. The psalm writer was describing the way God *acts*. This is another example of concrete words being used to describe an abstract thought. Below are a few more concrete words used to describe actions of God, who is spirit.

> The *eye* represents God's ability to "see" (Zech. 12:4).
> The *ear* represents God's ability to "hear" (2 Kings 19:16).
> God's *mouth* and the *voice* of God represent God's ability to "communicate" (Matt. 4:4; Num. 7:89).
> The *face* of God represents coming into "God's presence" (Gen. 32:30).
> His *hands* represent God's ability to "act" (Ps. 8:6).
> His *arm* represents God's "power in judgment" (Isa. 30:30).
> His *feet* represent God's ability to "move" (2 Sam. 22:10).

The Hebrews knew that God was the eternal, creative Spirit. There are several Old Testament references to the Spirit of God, such as: "The hand of the LORD was upon me, and he brought me out by the *Spirit* of the LORD..." (Ezek. 37:1a NIV, emphasis added).

In the New Testament, Jesus said clearly, "God is *spirit*, and his worshipers must worship in spirit and in truth." (John 4:24 NIV, emphasis added).

They knew that God was a spirit and consequently had no body parts. But they used those figures of speech listed above to express how God acted.

Why didn't they say what they meant? Why not say that God can *hear*, *see*, and *act*, if that is what they meant? They were following the style of thinking and speaking that was common in their culture, and their language was very *concrete*!

The Hebrews had no intention of describing the appearance of God with these figures of speech. They knew better. *We* are the ones who are misunderstanding! If we mean something concrete, we use a concrete word; if we mean something abstract, we use an abstract word. So we wrongly suppose that they could do the same. In reality, their whole language was very concrete, even when they described things we call abstract.

In summary, God is a Spirit. God is much more than can be contained in a body. He has no body to describe! The *Dictionary of Biblical Imagery* says, "The best thing we can do with these references is simply accept them as pictures of supernatural reality, full of mystery and the otherworldly."[1]

We may think of the Hebrew statement as more poetic, but in reality it was the *only way* they had to express the thought. The Hebrew approach required many more words to paint their "picture." The Greek/Western approach is much more efficient, since it uses fewer, more abstract, precise words.

Now that we realize that these are not logical arguments, how do we deal with them? First, allow yourself to *feel the picture at an emotional level*. Move from left brain to right brain. Instead of trying to follow every point of an argument, allow yourself to be involved in the pictures. Immerse yourself in them. Wallow around in them. Let them saturate your being. Delight in them. Let them wash over your soul and spirit. Let them do for you what the writer was allowing them to do for him. Let God touch you with them.

Now we come upon a major problem. The word pictures of the Hebrews that we find in the Bible are truth, but they are not in a form with which we are comfortable. As we read or hear a Hebrew word picture, we usually—without realizing that we are doing it—instantly try to *translate* it into our Greek, logical-sentence way of thinking. (Do you ever remember thinking, "I wonder what that means"? At that moment, you were trying to translate the picture into your familiar pattern of thinking!)

Here's the problem. Person A translates the picture one way, person B another, and person C still another way. For example, look at this picture: "Then Jesus came from Galilee to the Jordan to be baptized by John. But John tried to deter him, saying, 'I need to be baptized by you, and do you come to me?'¶ Jesus replied, 'Let it be so now; it is proper for us to do this to fulfill all righteousness.' Then John consented.¶ As soon as Jesus was baptized, he went up out of the water." (Matt. 3:13–16a. NIV).

The word picture here is *baptism*. Practically all Christians would accept the account above. The problem comes in the next step after reading or hearing the account. Usually, *unaware*, we translate this picture into our own way of thinking. We see "baptism" and instantly translate that word. Person A translates it into "immersion." Person B translates it into "pouring." And person C translates it into "sprinkling." And each one is instantly positive that he or she has it right.

This unconscious act of mental translation becomes the source of problems in understanding the Bible. This word picture of Jesus' submission to the will of the Father becomes for us a set of rules that must be agreed to and obeyed in every particular. The thought is: "Obviously I have it right and the other person has it wrong!"

Let's look at one more example. The big picture of Revelation shows God's judgment falling on the forces of evil: "Then I heard the angel in charge of the waters say:¶ 'You are just in these *judgments*, you who are and who were, the Holy One, because you have so *judged*;

for they have shed the blood of your saints and prophets, and you have given them blood to drink as they deserve.'¶ And I heard the altar respond: 'Yes, Lord God Almighty, true and just are your *judgments*.'" (Rev. 16:5–7 NIV, emphasis added).

Later, Jesus is shown returning as the cosmic King: "I saw heaven standing open and there before me was a white horse, whose rider is called Faithful and True. With justice he judges and makes war. His eyes are like blazing fire, and on his head are many crowns. He has a name written on him that no one knows but he himself. He is dressed in a robe dipped in blood, and his name is the Word of God." (Rev. 19:11–13 NIV).

And finally we see God making everything new and good: "And I heard a loud voice from the throne saying, 'Now the dwelling of God is with men, and he will live with them. They will be his people, and God himself will be with them and be their God. He will wipe every tear from their eyes. There will be no more death or mourning or crying or pain, for the old order of things has passed away.' He who was seated on the throne said, 'I am making everything new!'" (Rev. 21:3-5a NIV).

Looking at these accounts, practically all Christians would agree that the Scripture of Revelation is correct. But here we go again! As soon as we read or hear it, we respond with, "I wonder what that means!," and we begin to translate it into our pattern of thought. As Greek thinkers, we have a strong desire to sequence everything possible. So we try to make a time line of these word pictures. Inevitably, there are disagreements in the sequencing. Supporters of one view or another form entire movements. Arguments and divisions follow. Unintentionally, *we fail the Lord, who prayed for our unity as believers.*

What can we do? Ideally, we would learn to see these pictures as the Hebrews did. But I doubt that most people can stop translating into their own way of thinking. After all, it is our best, most comfortable way to think.

However, we *can* learn to:

1. Recognize that we are *translating* a picture of Scripture.
2. Acknowledge that there could be translation problems. (See chapter 37.)
3. Acknowledge that my translation might not be the final, best understanding.
4. Acknowledge that someone else might translate it better.
5. Therefore, be humble about having the whole truth.

We would be well-served to learn the Hebrew attitude of humility regarding things of God. James Sire wrote, "A recognition of our own proneness to error should be part of every Christian's world-view."[1]

We have to beware that we have not thoughtlessly picked up the Greek attitude that we can know all things! Humility does not mean that our faith is wobbly. It means that we know our limits.

To summarize, we must not presume that word pictures of the Hebrews and our logical sentences are interchangeable. We have to treat word pictures as what they are—no more and no less!

Paint me a picture in words. Tell me a story. Then don't spoil it by defining it!

CHAPTER 26

HOW CAN I DEAL WITH THEIR STORIES?

"Do you suppose the people of Israel really crossed the Red Sea on dry ground, and then the Egyptian army was swallowed up by the water?" queried Phil. "Or is that just a fairy tale kind of thing?"

"It certainly is not like anything I've ever experienced," Jody replied. "It seems to me that the story is telling of a miracle God did to save His people."

Are we dealing with tall tales of the same kind as Paul Bunyan? Are these rare exploits? Did God intervene to preserve his people from annihilation? Was there really a Goliath that David killed with a slingshot? What are we to make of these Bible stories?

Everybody loves a storyteller. Before Gutenberg's printing press moved print to the masses in 1456, storytellers were at every gathering. America embraced Mark Twain, with his *Tom Sawyer* and *Huckleberry Finn*, as our national storyteller in the nineteenth century. In the century that followed, Garrison Keeler held audiences spellbound with his tales of Lake Wobegon.

Large portions of our Bible are narrative accounts, stories. Always, they tell of God interacting with the Hebrew people. Here's an example:

Samuel summoned the people of Israel to the LORD at Mizpah and said to them, "This is what the LORD, the God of Israel, says: 'I brought Israel up out of Egypt, and I delivered you from the power of Egypt and all the kingdoms that oppressed you.' But you have now rejected your God, who saves you out of all your calamities and distresses. And you have said, 'No, set a king over us.' So now present yourselves before the LORD by your tribes and clans." ¶ When Samuel brought all the tribes of Israel near, the tribe of Benjamin was chosen. Then he brought forward the tribe of Benjamin, clan by clan, and Matri's clan was chosen. Finally Saul son of Kish was chosen. But when they looked for him, he was not to be found. So they inquired further of the LORD, "Has the man come here yet?"¶ And the LORD said, "Yes, he has hidden himself among the baggage."¶ They ran and brought him out, and as he stood among the people he was a head taller than any of the others. Samuel said to all the people, "Do you see the man the LORD has chosen? There is no one like him among all the people."¶ Then the people shouted, "Long live the king!" (1 Sam. 10:17–24 NIV)

This is the account in which the Hebrew people rejected Jehovah God as their king. They wanted an earthly king just like the surrounding nations. So God stepped aside and allowed them to have what they wanted.

We should not expect Greek accuracy in the details of their story. The Hebrew purpose is to make a point. They often left out many details that we would find important. Why? It is hard for us to realize, but print was very expensive in those days. (We discussed this in chapter 19.) Only the most important words, those necessary to carry the account, were written. This is not to say that their narratives are inaccurate, just that they often chose to leave out details that we would like to have.

These omissions or differences in style have caused some people to feel that the Bible is not trustworthy. On that point Grant Jeffrey has written: "Can we trust the Bible? The answer is an overwhelming *yes*! The reason for this confident statement is that for the past one hundred and fifty years many brilliant scholars have conducted detailed archeological examinations at thousands of sites throughout the Middle East. The results of their discoveries have proven that the Bible is reliable and accurate in every single area where its statements could be tested."[1]

During the late 1800s and the early 1900s, there were many scholars who doubted the accuracy of many details given in the Old Testament. They even questioned whether there had really been a King David. Grant Jeffrey responds: "Recent archeological investigations have demolished the position of those who rejected the biblical account of Israel's kings such as King David. In 1993, archeologists digging at Tel Dan in the Galilee in northern Israel found a fragment of a stone inscription that clearly refers to the 'house of David' and identifies David as the 'king of Israel.'"[2]

Some skeptics once questioned whether the Hittites ever existed. Since then, numerous discoveries have established the historical reality of the Hittite people. Such examples are many.

Storytellers carried the history of a people and established them as a community. The memory of the community guaranteed the accuracy of the narrative.

I do not like to use the word "stories" when referring to Bible accounts. Many people think of a story as a fairy tale, something totally fabricated. The accounts of the Bible are not fabricated, not made-up stories. They are accurate accounts of events from many years ago. Yes, they are in a form that is a little different from what we use now, but that does not make them inaccurate. Therefore, I accept the accounts of the Bible as historically accurate.

CHAPTER 27

IS THE BIBLE LOGICAL OR NOT?

"That just doesn't seem logical to me," Jody charged. "Should I be expected to believe something that is so illogical?"

"You ask questions that I don't know how to answer," responded Phil.

Logic is not the only approach to finding truth. There are other ways to solve problems.

When our granddaughter Arah was in grade school, I became exasperated with her approach to a new computer program. *I* would sit back and study the screen, trying to understand the logic of the program. But not Arah! She would dive right in and start pushing buttons. I would say, "You are going to break something." But she never did. She proved me wrong. Guess who knows how to operate a computer better today. Right! She does.

As a whole, *the Bible is illogical.* How can I say that? How can truth be presented without logic?

The answer is easy to understand, but it is not obvious. What we call *logic* began in Greece. It was started by Aristotle, who lived between 382 BC and 322 BC. His students developed it further. The Greek language and logic spread into the Near East with the conquests of Alexander the Great at about the same time. The influence of logic obviously took effect first in the universities among the scholars and slowly spread out to the general population.

What we call logic had no effect on the general population of areas in which the Bible was written—until shortly *after* the time of Christ. This means that the entire Old Testament was written before what we call logic came into existence. Only about 10 percent of the Bible was affected by logic—all in the later writings of the New Testament.

The letters of Paul in the New Testament were the first part of the Bible to use our logic. The Thessalonian letters were among the earliest writings of the New Testament, written around AD 50–51. It is easy to see that Paul, being an intellectual in the city of Tarsus (the seat of a major university and not so far across the Mediterranean from Greece), would have been quickly affected by the new logic. One of his most famous passages—one that uses beautiful logic is found in the "love chapter": 1 Corinthians 13.

The gospel of John appears to have been written between AD 85–95. It was written for the Gentile church, and though it is Hebrew in mind-set, it is very Greek in its thought and logic. James Sire wrote: "The Gospel of John shows him [Jesus] in long discourses, in some of which he uses ordinary human reasoning that follows the standard patterns of logic."[1]

The letter we call Hebrews uses our logic with the subject matter of the Old Testament. It argues that Jesus is the fulfillment of the sacrifice system and the priesthood of the law of Moses. It is a mixture of Hebrew material presented with Greek logic.

The little letters just before Revelation were written by Peter, John, and Jude. All use our form of reasoning. So it seems that our logic had begun to affect the general population by the time of their writing. The book of 1 Peter was the first of these, being written about AD 64, and the others came later.

The conclusion is that our form of Greek logic had begun to reach into the Gentile church in the letters of Paul by about AD 50.

Before our logic was available to the Bible writers, how did they present their message? They sometimes used narrative and sometimes used what I call "word pictures."

Narrative, or a story line, needs no explanation. It is straightforward. The account of God creating a path through the Red Sea illustrates narrative:

Then the LORD said to Moses, "Stretch out your hand over the sea so that the waters may flow back over the Egyptians and their chariots and horsemen." Moses stretched out his hand over the sea, and at daybreak the sea went back to its place. The Egyptians were fleeing toward it, and the LORD swept them into the sea. The water flowed back and covered the chariots and horsemen—the entire army of Pharaoh that had followed the Israelites into the sea. Not one of them survived.¶ But the Israelites went through the sea on dry ground, with a wall of water on their right and on their left. That day the LORD saved Israel from the hands of the Egyptians, and Israel saw the Egyptians lying dead on the shore. And when the Israelites saw the great power the LORD displayed against the Egyptians, the people feared the LORD and put their trust in him and in Moses his servant. (Ex. 14:26–31 NIV).

A large part of the Bible is simple narrative. This is not reasoned argument, but it does make sense. It is simply telling the story. However, I need to stress that their narrative and ours is different. Because of the extreme expense of writing in that day, they used only the necessary words to carry the story line. We expect much more detail to be given.

Next we will look at word pictures. Word pictures are nothing more than mental pictures painted by words. They are descriptive. After reading a word picture, the reader has a mental image in his or her mind. For example, "Many bulls surround me; strong bulls of Bashan encircle me." (Ps. 22:12 NIV) is a picture of feeling surrounded as by threatening bulls.

"Roaring lions tearing their prey open their mouths wide against me." (Ps. 22:13 NIV). The writer feels like a gladiator about to face wild lions.

"I am poured out like water, and all my bones are out of joint." (Ps. 22:14a NIV). His strength has gone away like water poured on the ground. His muscles are useless, since his bones are all dislocated.

"My heart has turned to wax; it has melted away within me." (Ps. 22:14b NIV). His inner being is no longer working; it's gone.

"My strength is dried up like a potsherd, and my tongue sticks to the roof of my mouth; you lay me in the dust of death." (Ps. 22:15 NIV). His strength is shattered like a piece of broken pottery. He has no saliva. He feels like he is already cremated.

"Dogs have surrounded me; a band of evil men has encircled me, they have pierced my hands and my feet." (Ps. 22:16 NIV). These dogs are the wild ones that ran in packs. They are moving in for the kill. Already they have his hands and feet.

"I can count all my bones; people stare and gloat over me." (Ps. 22:17 NIV). He looks like a starved person. He sees the crowd making fun of his death.

"They divide my garments among them and cast lots for my clothing." (Ps. 22:18 NIV). He no longer has need for clothing, so they are gambling to see who gets them.

Are these examples descriptive? Wow! Can't you feel the anguish of the writer's soul after reading those few verses? No wonder Jesus picked from this psalm to express how he felt on the cross of Calvary. This shows us the punch that is possible by using a word picture.

While writing this material, I discovered a book that makes my point exactly. It is the *Dictionary of Biblical Imagery*. This work contains over one thousand pages, 850 articles—all talking about the images (which I call *word pictures*) of the Bible.

On the front flyleaf, Haddon Robinson wrote, "People think with pictures in their heads. The Bible is God's picture book, even though it is all in words."[2] In the introduction, the editors wrote, "The Bible is more than a book of ideas: it is also a book of images and motifs. Everywhere we turn we find concrete pictures and recurrent patterns."[3] I highly recommend this book for any serious student of the Bible.

One more thought about logic. What is the subject of the Bible? It's God, of course. Can God be contained in human words? That is a foolish thought, isn't it? God is far bigger than humanity or any human language. Our attempts to think and talk about God are so very limited. Therefore, why would anyone expect that God could possibly be contained in logic? That is a nonsensical idea, but it is thoughtlessly held by many people!

We should study the Bible with Hebrew humility, which says that we can only know about God what he chooses to reveal to us. This has been revealed in different types of thought patterns. Much of that revelation has been given in Hebrew word pictures and narrative. The parts of the Bible that use the Greek thought patterns that we are so familiar with are the gospel of John, the letter to the Hebrews, Paul's letters, and the little letters before Revelation.

This brief survey should show us the power and clarity of language the Hebrews had available to them long before what we call logic came into existence.

The Bible is mostly prelogic. The charge is true that most of the Bible does not use the logic we find most comfortable. The Bible uses mostly Hebrew narrative and word pictures to powerfully bring its message.

CHAPTER 28

WHY ARE THESE WORDS SO DIFFERENT?

"A person is like a tree or like chaff. I don't get it," Jody fretted. "Why doesn't the Bible just say the person is prosperous or worthless or whatever. Why beat around the bush like that?"

"It doesn't make any sense to me either," Phil replied. "I don't know why they talked like that."

Have you ever posed a problem to a friend and begun to talk about it with them? After a while, you might have discovered that the person didn't understand your question and was thinking along another line entirely. My response to this situation is something like "Whoa! We are not on the same page at all! Let's start over."

This lack of communication is very confusing. It must be solved. "Not being on the same page" often happens to us when we are reading the Bible. Why?

The culture of the Hebrews was very different from ours, and not just in technology or their customs. The Hebrews who wrote the Bible did not *think* the way we do!

R. C. Sproul wrote: "Unless we maintain that the Bible fell down from heaven on a parachute, inscribed by a heavenly pen in a peculiar heavenly language uniquely suited as a vehicle for divine revelation, or that the Bible was dictated directly and immediately by God without reference to any local custom, style or perspective, we are going to have to face the culture gap. That is, the Bible reflects the culture of its day."[1]

The culture, language, and even thinking of the Bible's writers are very different from ours. Hebrew society was very different from what we know. These were people who lived very close to the earth. Their lives depended on the success of the crops, and those crops depended on the rains. If they had a drought, starvation was at the door.

We constantly stress the accuracy of a statement by saying that it is scientific. But the people of the Bible knew nothing of what we call science. The writing of the Bible was finished by AD 120. What we call science did not begin until 1543, when Copernicus published his *On the Revolutions of the Heavenly Spheres.* He was quickly followed by John Newton's studies of gravity, light, motion, and so on. Our Bible writers wrote with the understanding of their day, which was prescientific.

They also knew nothing of what we call logic. They had a form of logic that seems strange to us. We have trouble following it. So, naturally, their language developed to express *their* way of thinking. Since their thinking was concrete, their language was also concrete. King David wrote what I call a word picture in the Psalm 1:3: "He *is like* a *tree* planted by *streams of water,* which yields its *fruit* in *season* and whose *leaf* does not wither. Whatever he does prospers." (Ps. 1:3 NIV, emphasis added).

Notice the phrase *is like*. This psalm is a comparison. It is a word picture in *concrete* language about a person who lives in right relationship with God. Note the concrete words: *tree, water, fruit, season*, and *leaf*. This word picture is used as a comparison to a spiritual relationship.

In contrast, the Greek or Westerner might say about the same person: "He will persist and flourish." This is the same idea expressed in our *abstract* language.

The Hebrews did not have the words *persist* or *flourish*. We may think of the Hebrew statement as more poetic, but in reality it was the *only way they had* to express the thought. The Hebrew approach requires many more words to paint their picture. Our Greek/Western approach is much more efficient, since it uses fewer, more abstract, and more precise words.

The way any culture thinks dictates the language it develops. The Hebrews' thinking was *concrete,* so naturally their language was also *concrete.* Their language referred to *actual things or actions*: trees, streams, rocks, water, fighting, harvesting.

We are thoroughly Greek/Western in our thinking. We think *abstractly.* We can't help it. We are that way because our entire educational system and culture has saturated us with the Greek/ Western approach. Consequently, our language has many *abstract* words. These words express an idea *without relating to a real object or action*, such as: beauty, justice, humor, honesty.

The Hebrews described "bulging eyes and flaring nostrils" (all *concrete* words). To express the same idea, we say "angry" (an *abstract* word).

Hebrews used "arm" to express what we call "strength" or "power," (Isa. 59:1).

They used "blind"; we say "ignorance," (Isa. 29:18).

They used "crown"; we say "victory," (James 1:12).

They used "fat"; we say "abundance," (Jer. 5:28).

They used "fire"; we say "judgment," (Ps. 21:9).

They used "gate"; we say "security," (Ps. 147:13).

They used "key"; we say "authority," (Rev. 1:18).

They used "rock"; we say "refuge," (Ps. 18:2).

Even the word "love," which we view as an abstract word, for the Hebrews originally referred to the sexual relationship—obviously a very concrete action.

This tendency to be very *concrete* may strike us as poetic, but in reality they did not have the *abstract* words available to them that we use so readily.

Even today, we enjoy the Hebrews' concrete word pictures so much, because they appeal to the right side of our brain. Instead of analyzing them, we relish the beauty of the images the word pictures present. The *Dictionary of Biblical Imagery* says: "Pictures affect us emotionally in ways that abstractions do not."[2]

So, when the Hebrews tried to talk about spiritual things, they were forced to refer to *abstract* realities—such as God, angels, or heaven—using *concrete* words. *We need to realize that these concrete words cannot possibly carry the weight assigned to them.* But that was as close as they could get!

The point of this chapter is that the Hebrew authors were forced to use *concrete* words to talk about *abstract* realities. The *Dictionary of*

Biblical Imagery says: "This dictionary will show that concrete images lie behind many of the abstractions in modern English translations of the Bible."[3]

What most of us forget is that all language at that time was mostly communicated by talking and listening. Reading and writing were not available to most people. Those skills were performed by a scribe. His position was necessary for any writing or reading that involved more than single words or phrases. Because we live in a literate society, we presume that all people can read and write. However, in my experience as a speech/language pathologist, I have often asked people how much they read and write. Often I have been told, "Not much." On probing, I found that they only read single words, such as signs, and wrote things like grocery lists. They wouldn't ever try to write a letter. These same people "read" the newspaper by scanning the headlines only. So we should not be so surprised by an ancient society in which reading and writing was limited in the same way.

Since the Hebrews thought so differently from the way we do, we should expect that they used different patterns to express themselves. And they did.

We expect abstract thought and language that was not available to the Bible writers. Our expectation is not reasonable. Their language was concrete. They knew only basic, concrete words.

This next statement is very important: we unconsciously change their words from *concrete* to *abstract*, into our way of thinking. We need to become aware of our mental translation as we read Hebrew material. We must become aware of the way we try to put their way of thinking into ours.

To better understand the Bible, we need to try to think as the Hebrews did!

CHAPTER 29

WHY DO THEY REPEAT THEMSELVES SO MUCH?

"I get so tired of those people saying the same thing over and over," complained Jody. "Can't they remember when they've already said something?"

"Do you think they actually forgot?" Phil asked. "I don't know."

Having worked with the elderly population for years, I was not surprised when I heard Uncle John repeat his last deer hunting story. He had already forgotten that he had just told it a few minutes earlier. When he told it the third time, I listened with interest, but I said to myself, "He's really losing it!" Before we left that afternoon, he told the same story two more times. On the way home, I told Eileen about the five repetitions, and we agreed that he was really failing and probably wouldn't live much longer. He did die soon afterward.

Being saturated with the Greek approach to life, we do not take kindly to people who repeat themselves very much. Our reaction is that they are wasting our time. However, we do use repetition for emphasis: for example, "Stop! Stop!" or "Yes, yes!"

It is a big error to presume that we think the same way the Hebrews of the Bible did. We Greek/Westerners love the logical sequence of our material. We expect points one, two, three, four, five, and so on. We expect each subsequent statement to build on the ones before and finally reach a stated conclusion.

But Hebrews did not think that way. Because the Hebrew language had a relatively small vocabulary, and to be sure their listener understood, they learned to present *the same idea in several ways.* This is called *parallelism: one idea in several different forms, using different words.* These Hebrew statements are parallel, not different.

One of the best known examples of parallelism is found in Psalm 23.

The LORD is my shepherd, I shall not be in want. He makes me lie down in green pastures, he leads me beside quiet waters, he restores my soul. He guides me in paths of righteousness for his name's sake. Even though I walk through the valley of the shadow of death, I will fear no evil, for you are with me; your rod and your staff, they comfort me.¶ You prepare a table before me in the presence of my enemies. You anoint my head with oil; my cup overflows. Surely goodness and love will follow me all the days of my life, and I will dwell in the house of the LORD forever." (Ps. 23:1–6 NIV).

Clearly, the point of the psalm is this: "I shall not be in want" (NIV). *The Living Bible* translates it, "I have everything I need!" The remainder of the psalm is not different from this initial statement but is an elaboration on it.

This psalm is not *in sequence*; it is an extreme form of *parallelism.*

Our Greek/Western mind tends to be satisfied with an abstract statement and is ready to move on to the next abstract statement. But it is also clear that we find great satisfaction in the elaboration, because Psalm 23 is one of the best-known and most-loved of all passages in the Bible.

You can turn to many parts of our Bible and find this device in use. Let me share another example from the Old Testament in Isaiah 40:1–5 (NIV).

Comfort, comfort my people, says your God.	(*first thought*)
Speak tenderly to Jerusalem,	(repeated)
and proclaim to her	
that her hard service has been completed,	(repeated)
that her sin has been paid for,	(repeated)
that she has received from the LORD's hand	(repeated)
double for all her sins.	
A voice of one calling:	(*second thought*)
"In the desert prepare	
the way for the LORD;	
make straight in the wilderness	(repeated)
a highway for our God.	
Every valley shall be raised up,	(repeated)
every mountain and hill made low;	(repeated)
the rough ground shall become level,	(repeated)
the rugged places a plain.	(repeated)
And the glory of the LORD will be revealed,	(*third thought*)
and all mankind together will see it.	(repeated)
For the mouth of the LORD has spoken.	(*fourth thought*)

The Greek way of giving the same message would be something like this: "Give my people a message of comfort. Get ready for God's deliverance to come. Everybody will see the glory of God."

We may be very comfortable with our newer Greek form, but it certainly lacks the beauty and power of the older Hebrew method.

Let's look at more from the teachings of Jesus in the New Testament.

Anyone who loves his father or mother more than me is not worthy of me (*first thought*); anyone who loves his son or daughter more than me is not worthy of me (repeated); and anyone who does not take his cross and follow me is not worthy of me (repeated) (Matt. 10:37–38 NIV).

Come to me, all you who are weary and burdened, and I will give you rest (*first thought*). Take my yoke upon you and learn from me, for I am gentle and humble in heart, and you will find rest for your souls (repeated). For my yoke is easy and my burden is light (repeated) (Matt. 11:28–30 NIV).

I hope you can see the power, the beauty, and the clarity that is produced by the Hebrew repetition of an initial idea.

Most importantly, we must *not* think that Hebrew writers are presenting a new thought each time we see a new phrase or sentence. Certainly, our Greek way has taught us to expect a new thought, but when reading Hebrew material, we must hold that Greek expectation in check. When reading our Bible, *we must expect repetition, or parallelism.*

I remember hearing a pastor labor for a half hour or so on the difference between *sin* and *iniquity*. In reality, there is no difference. They are two forms of the same abstract thought (rebellion against God). *Sin* and *iniquity*, used together, are a very common example of

Hebrew parallelism found in our Bible: "I will punish their *sin* with the rod, their *iniquity* with flogging" (Ps. 89:32 NIV).

The *Dictionary of Biblical Imagery* says, "We should not allow the simplicity of this type of balance (parallelism) to obscure how much of the Bible is based on it: the prophetic books and wisdom literature of the Bible, as well as the discourses of Jesus, rely on the biblical verse form of parallelism."[1]

We repeat ourselves for emphasis. They repeated themselves, with different words, so the meaning would be clear.

CHAPTER 30

WHY ISN'T THE BIBLE SCIENTIFIC?

"Do you remember thinking that the moon was made of green cheese?" queried Jody.

"Well, yeah, but that was when I was a little kid, and Armstrong hadn't walked on it yet," agreed Phil.

A recent TV ad presents a high school student demonstrating his science project by gripping and emptying a paper cup of water with a robot arm. The lad says, "Isn't that cool?" The ad concludes with the banner: Science Rules.

That ad pretty well summarizes our attitude toward science. We feel that science has all the answers. But it doesn't.

Science does solve huge problems, so long as those problems deal with matter: transportation, communication, health care, finance, and so on. But has science solved the political problems in our nation or in the world? Has science solved the dilemma of inhumanity toward humanity? Has science created better marriages? Has it developed the solution to a broken heart?

It's true that our bodies are made of matter. But people are more than matter. The Bible affirms: "May God himself, the God of peace, sanctify you through and through. May your whole spirit, soul and body be kept blameless at the coming of our Lord Jesus Christ." (1 Thess. 5:23 NIV).

Notice that this verse lists *spirit, soul,* and *body.* We are three-part beings. In many passages, the Bible affirms that we are much more than the matter that composes our body. The gospel of John refers to the body as a temporary dwelling place, like a tent. I recall my Greek professor stressing the temporary, tent-like quality of the body when referring to John 1:14. I found this well presented only in the *Amplified Bible.*

And the Word (Christ) became flesh (human, incarnate) and tabernacled (*fixed His tent of flesh*, lived awhile) among us; and we [actually] saw His glory (His honor, His majesty), such glory as an only begotten son receives from his father, full of grace (favor, loving-kindness) and truth. (John 1:14 AB).

The "fixed his tent of flesh" phrase expresses the biblical view that the body is a temporary dwelling made of matter. The real and permanent "you" is your spirit and soul.

Science has not been able to find or deal with this reality of the spirit. Many people whose philosophy of life (worldview) is based on science have simply decided that there is no such thing as *spirit.* As Del Tackett so pointedly says, "They will only consider what is *in* the box."[1] No consideration is given to where the box came from or why it is here. *The ultimate questions are beyond science.*

Therefore, since the Bible is a spiritual book, we need to be especially alert so that we do not fall into the trap of requiring scientific proof. The Bible consistently presents a Creator God who is above and beyond his creation.

"In the beginning God created the heavens and the earth." (Gen. 1:1 NIV). He is not bound by the laws of nature. He created them. He can at any point overrule them. To think otherwise is to say that the Creator is now ruled by the machine that he created. It's a foolish thought, isn't it? The Creator that brought all into being is still in charge. He can do whatever he chooses to do.

When he does things that obviously go against the laws of nature, we call that a miracle. Most doctors I know will tell you that they have seen miracles. Both my wife and I have seen miracles. (We were in the company of forty thousand people when we closely witnessed a man blinded by *retinitis pigmentosa* receive his sight. I talked with him the next day, as he was relearning to walk as a sighted person.) Yes, God still overrules his laws for the benefit of his people.

Science can only study the creation, not the Creator.

Science deals with the laws of nature. But you and I are more than a mass of connected cells that will one day die. God has given us, through Jesus Christ, the potential to be in fellowship with him.

To understand the Bible you will have to concede that God can do the supernatural. Humanity is the peak of his creation, but he is the Creator and ruler of all. The Bible is the record of his revealing himself to us.

I suggest that you read *The Reason for God: Belief in an Age of Skepticism* by Timothy Keller.

CHAPTER 31

WHERE IS THE CONCLUSION OF THIS PARABLE?

"Did you make any sense of that vineyard owner paying all the workers the same?" Phil asked. "Some of them worked twelve times more than the others. That's not fair."

"Well, certainly God is fair," Jody replied. "But no, I don't get it either."

Jody and Phil are not alone. For all of my adult life I have had the vague feeling that I was not really understanding the parables of Jesus. Now I know why! I was naturally using the conventions of *our* culture to try to understand the culture of Bible times. When we stop to think about it, that approach is silly! Cultures change constantly. The music of our grandparents is of little interest to our children. Words used to be spelled out completely, and now we abbreviate everything possible. Even English grammar has changed radically since I went to high school. Where today do any of us use "should" or "whom"? So, why would any of us expect that the cultural conventions we use will work on material from several thousand years ago—and half a world away?

One of our cultural conventions is the expectation of finding the conclusion of an argument at the *end*. Of course it belongs at the end. The word *conclusion* means "end"! But that is not what the Hebrews did.

How do I know? Kenneth Bailey lived and taught in the Middle East for over forty years. Living there, he absorbed the culture, language, and social conventions of the area. He came to see that we were missing much of the impact of Jesus' life and teachings. He has published his insights in *Jesus through Middle Eastern Eyes*.[1] Let's apply his understandings to several parables of Jesus.

Be dressed ready for service and keep your lamps burning, like men waiting for their master to return from a wedding banquet, so that when he comes and knocks they can immediately open the door for him. It will be good for those servants whose master finds them watching when he comes. I tell you the truth, he will dress himself to serve, will have them recline at the table and will come and wait on them. It will be good for those servants whose master finds them ready, even if he comes in the second or third watch of the night. But understand this: If the owner of the house had known at what hour the thief was coming, he would not have let his house be broken into. You also must be ready, because the Son of Man will come at an hour when you do not expect him. (Luke 12:35–40 NIV).

Using our Greek convention, we would look at the end to find the climax, the point of the parable. To us it looks like, *we need to be ready*. That certainly is part of the message. But the Hebrews were used to the pattern the prophets used. For them the shocker is found near the middle of the message, at the end of verse 37, which says: "It will be good for those servants whose master finds them watching when he comes. I tell you the truth, *he will dress himself to serve, will have them recline at the table and will come and wait on them.*"

Let's think of this passage as a peanut butter and jelly sandwich.

Verses 35 and 36 are introduction (the wrapper). The servants are blessed (the upper slice of bread). The master comes and finds them (still the upper slice).

The master prepares and serves the servants. This is the point—the peanut butter and jelly filling!

The master comes and finds the servants (the lower slice of bread). The servants are blessed (still the lower slice).

Verses 39 and 40 are application (the other side of the wrapper).

Notice the ascending order: The upper slice moves to the point of the parable, the filling, and then to the lower slice. At the end is the application. The point of the parable, *the good stuff,* is in the middle.

Was Jesus saying that *the Master serves the servants?* This was unheard of! Jesus was really teaching about the nature of God. He was saying that God cares so much for his people that he came to us in order to *serve us* in the person of Jesus. Can we see the entire parable echoed when Jesus washed the disciples' feet—and then went to the cross to pay our sin debt?

Let's look at the illustration commonly called the parable of the prodigal son.

Jesus continued: "There was a man who had two sons. The younger one said to his father, 'Father, give me my share of the estate.' So he divided his property between them. ¶ Not long after that, the younger son got together all he had, set off for a distant country and there squandered his wealth in wild living. After he had spent everything, there was a severe famine in that whole country, and he began to be in need. So he went and hired himself out to a citizen of that country, who sent him to his fields to feed pigs. He longed to fill his stomach with the pods that the pigs were eating, but no one gave him anything. ¶ When he came to his senses, he said, 'How many of my father's hired men have food to spare, and here I am starving to death! I will set out and go back to my father and say to him: Father, I have sinned against heaven and against you. I am no longer worthy to be called your son; make me like one of your hired men.' So he got up and went to his father.¶ But while he was still a long way off, his father saw him and was filled with compassion for him; he ran to his son, threw his arms around him and kissed him. ¶ The son said to him, 'Father, I have sinned against heaven and against you. I am no longer worthy to be called your son.' ¶ But the father said to his servants, 'Quick! Bring the best robe and put it on him. Put a ring on his finger and sandals on his feet. Bring the fattened calf and kill it. Let's have a feast and celebrate. For this son of mine was dead and is alive again; he was lost and is found.' So they began to celebrate.¶ Meanwhile, the older son was in the field. When he came near the house, he heard music and dancing. So he called one of the servants and asked him what was going on. 'Your brother has come,' he replied, 'and your father has killed the fattened calf because he has him back safe and sound.' ¶ The older brother became angry and refused to go in. So his father went out and pleaded with him. But he answered his father, 'Look! All these years I've been slaving for you and never disobeyed your orders. Yet you never gave me even a young goat so I could celebrate with my friends. But when this son of yours who has squandered your property with prostitutes comes home, you kill the fattened calf for him!' ¶ 'My son,' the father said, 'you are always with me, and everything I have is yours. But we had to celebrate and be glad, because this brother of yours was dead and is alive again; he was lost and is found.'" (Luke 15:11–32 NIV).

Usually we feel that this is a story about a son who comes to his senses, and therefore it is called the parable of the prodigal son. However, if we look at this as the Hebrews did, we will find that the parable has a different point. *It is not about the son.* The peanut butter and jelly in the middle is about the *father.* Notice the ascending and descending structure.

The first part, the upper crust (ascending numbers 1–4 below), is about the sinners who hear Jesus gladly.

1. The young son takes his inheritance.
2. The young son wastes his money.
3. The young son comes to his senses.
4. The young son repents and returns home.
5. *The father fully reinstates the son.* (This is the point, the peanut butter and jelly.)
4. The older son is unrepentant.
3. The older son does not come to his senses.
2. The older son has the same attitude toward father's estate.
1. The older son also refuses to be part of the family.

The last part, the lower crust (descending numbers 4–1), is about the religious leaders who refuse to hear Jesus' message.

The good part is in the middle. For the Hebrew, this parable is about the *outrageous love of the Father.* What father in his right mind would accept back into good standing a son who had so hurt, so shamed him? But this father was *watching* for the son's return and *ran* to hug him! He had to get to the son before the villagers did, because they probably would have stoned him for bringing shame on the father and their village. Then he reinstated the son by giving him the best robe and sandals. He even gave this son the checkbook—the signet ring. Unbelievable!

Notice that the point of the parable is not at the end. As before, the good part of the parable is in the middle, with very important upper and lower crusts around it.

For one more example, let's turn to the passage in Matthew that Jody was complaining about.

For the kingdom of heaven is like a landowner who went out early in the morning to hire men to work in his vineyard. He agreed to pay them a denarius for the day and sent them into his vineyard. ¶ About the third hour he went out and saw others standing in the marketplace doing nothing. He told them, "You also go and work in my vineyard, and I will pay you whatever is right." So they went.¶ He went out again about the sixth hour and the ninth hour and did the same thing. About the eleventh hour he went out and found still others standing around. He asked them, "Why have you been standing here all day long doing nothing?" ¶ "Because no one has hired us," they answered.¶ He said to them, "You also go and work in my vineyard." ¶ When evening came, the owner of the vineyard said to his foreman, "Call the workers and pay them their wages, beginning with the last ones hired and going on to the first." ¶ The workers who were hired about the eleventh hour came and each received a denarius. So when those came who were hired first, they expected to receive more. But each one of them also received a denarius. When they received it, they began to grumble against the landowner. "These men who were hired last worked only one hour," they said, "and you have made them equal to us who have borne the burden of the work and the heat of the day."¶ But he answered one of them, "Friend, I am not being unfair to you. Didn't you agree to work for a denarius? Take your pay and go. I want to give the man who was hired last the same as I gave you. Don't I have the right to do what I want with my own money? Or are you envious because I am generous?" (Matt. 20:1–15 NIV).

We feel that the parable is about the workers not being paid proportionately. Our gut reaction to this parable agrees with the workers: "That's not fair!"

But the Hebrew way of looking at the parable gives this outline a different climax. Again, the good stuff is in the middle.

1. An agreement was made.
2. The master would pay just wages.
3. Workers were hired at the last hour.
4. *The same wage was paid to everyone.* (This is the point, the peanut butter and jelly.)
3. The last-hour workers received the just wage.
2. The first-hired workers expected to receive more.
1. The master kept his agreement.

The point for the Hebrew listener was that *the master* (God) *was so generous* and caring for those who could not find work to support their families, that he gave a full day's wage to those who only worked a single hour. This parable demonstrates that God loves not only those "good people" who appear to be deserving of their salvation, but also the "undeserving." It illustrates God's grace as favor that we cannot earn. This is discussed more fully in chapter 41).

As before, this parable is not about the workers but about the Master. And the conclusion is not at the end but somewhere near the middle.

When I've followed the social customs I grew up with in America and expected to find the climax of a story at the *end*, I often missed the point of Jesus' teaching! The point wasn't about *us*. It was about *the Master*!

What is so confusing to us Westerners is that *the patterns change*. Some parables *do* have the point at the end. For example, let's consider this parable.

Someone in the crowd said to him, "Teacher, tell my brother to divide
the inheritance with me." ¶ Jesus replied, "Man, who appointed me
a judge or an arbiter between you?" Then he said to them, "Watch
out! Be on your guard against all kinds of greed; a man's life does not
consist in the abundance of his possessions." ¶ And he told them this
parable: "The ground of a certain rich man produced a good crop.
He thought to himself, 'What shall I do? I have no place to store
my crops.' ¶ "Then he said, 'This is what I'll do. I will tear down my
barns and build bigger ones, and there I will store all my grain and
my goods. And I'll say to myself, "You have plenty of good things
laid up for many years. Take life easy; eat, drink and be merry."' ¶
"But God said to him, 'You fool! This very night your life will be
demanded from you. Then who will get what you have prepared for
yourself?' ¶ "This is how it will be with anyone who stores up things
for himself but is not rich toward God." (Luke 12:13–21 NIV).

In this parable the sequence is *one, two, three, four, climax*—just as
we expect.

Supporting our misunderstanding are the section titles that the
publishers have placed in many Bibles. These were never a part
of the original Hebrew or Greek text. They have been added for
the reader's convenience. However, *these subtitles follow our expected
Greek pattern rather than the Hebrew pattern*. Consequently, they
reinforce our misunderstanding.

The section title in my Bible for Luke 12:35 is "Watchfulness,"
implying that the point is that *we* are to watch. But the point really
is that *the Master is compassionate*!

The section title for Matthew 20:1 is "The Parable of the Workers in
the Vineyard," implying that it is about the *workers*. But the point
is that *the Master is showing great generosity*.

So keep in mind that the section titles in your Bible may be misleading, because they view the parables the Greek way. Don't place too much reliability on the titles.

This chapter has detailed the unexpected placement of the climax or moral of the story. Hebrews often placed the point of their story near the middle, not at the end as we expect. We must learn to look at the parables with Hebrew eyes.

Jesus taught with the pattern of the prophets. For us, that was long ago and far away.

CHAPTER 32

WHAT WAS THE HEBREW MIND-SET?

"Have you met that new girl from Iraq?" Jody asked. "She speaks pretty well, but she sure has funny ideas."

"What funny ideas does she have?" Phil asked.

"For example," Jody replied, "she doesn't want to date until she is ready to marry."

Jody was reacting to the new girl's mind-set. A *mind-set* is the collection of principles through which all of us view our world. "Cleanliness is next to godliness" is one example of a mind-set.

Mind-set has both positive and negative qualities.

My maternal grandparents were a hard-working and prosperous farm family in south-central Pennsylvania. The farm looked like a picture postcard: a beautiful, white-sideboard, two-story house with front and side porches, white outbuilding/summer kitchen and white woodshed, cast-iron fence near the road, and a picture-perfect garden. Of course, there was also a white outhouse. It was wallpapered inside and had felt liners on the seats. As expected, the big barn was sparkling white, with Center Cove Farm painted proudly on it.

As technology advanced, Grandpa installed a twelve-volt electrical system in the house, followed by indoor plumbing. Next came a bathtub, sink, and commode in the bathroom upstairs. But Grandpa was more comfortable using the outhouse, even in freezing weather. As long as his health allowed, he used the outhouse.

That is the power of mind-set.

The Hebrews had a mind-set also. Their theological mind-set went like this:

1. There is only one true God. All others are pretenders, false gods.
2. This one true God is holy (different), far beyond his creation.
3. God can only be known to the extent that he chooses to reveal himself.
4. God called Abram to obey his commands and promised that Abram would become a nation.
5. God called Moses to lead that nation and free it from slavery.
6. God gave the Ten Commandments to all people to reveal his nature.
7. The prophets spoke God's message, "Return to me or be judged!" The prophets also gave insights into God's nature.
8. The prophets told of a coming Messiah, the Anointed One, who would free them from oppression.

These understandings were standard across the Hebrew nation, even during times of rebellion against God.

In contrast, the mind-set of the Greeks was very different. The Greeks had many gods that were believed to have exaggerated human traits. They were simply overblown humans! Their loves were bigger, hatreds bigger, and actions bigger. Further, the Greeks believed that nothing was beyond the human mind and that their gods were just like them! Therefore, they felt they could know their gods totally.

Without realizing its source, we have picked up from the Greeks the attitude that we have the right to know everything—even God! What arrogance! *And we have picked up the attitude that our words, our theology, can contain all the truth of God.* Therefore, we feel that our statements of belief have every right to be rigid and unbending. This leads to attitudes that say, "I am right. You are wrong. You see it my way, or we cannot be in fellowship!"

We need to become aware of our *personal mind-set*. What are the principles by which we live? What do we really believe? What do we stand for? A large part of our maturity comes with knowing who we are.

PART VI

UNDERSTANDING THE BIBLE

CHAPTER 33

DO ALL PARTS OF THE BIBLE APPLY TO US NOW?

"I don't know if we are doing right nor not," Jody said apprehensively. "I read in the Bible that women were to keep their heads covered."

"I know what you mean," Phil responded. "I read there that a man is not to shave his beard either. I wonder why we don't pay attention to that."

Many people across the years have been troubled about what applies to whom and when. Do only some parts of the Bible apply to us? If so, which parts, and why?

The TV program *20/20* aired a segment on November 25, 2011, about the Westboro Baptist Church in Topeka, Kansas. This is a group that pickets military funerals, celebrity funerals, gay events, Jewish institutions, funerals of victims of AIDS, pop concerts, etc. They carry large posters that display statements such as: "Thank God

169

for 9/11," "Thank God for IEDs," "God is a terrorist," "God is angry every day," and so on.

Where did they get the idea for such protests? Their answer is that it is in the Bible. They can point to God's judgment of sin in the Bible.

Are we to stand in judgment as the Westboro church does? Is everything we find in the Bible of equal value? Does all of it apply to us now?

How about these?

"Do not wear clothing woven of two kinds of material." (Lev. 19:19d NIV). Every man's suit coat has one type of material on the outside and a smooth fabric lining on the inside.

"Do not cut the hair at the sides of your head or clip off the edges of your beard." (Lev. 19:27 NIV). My haircuts are always short on the sides, and I shave my beard entirely.

"If a man has a stubborn and rebellious son who does not obey his father and mother and will not listen to them when they discipline him, his father and mother shall take hold of him and bring him to the elders at the gate of his town. They shall say to the elders, 'This son of ours is stubborn and rebellious. He will not obey us. He is a profligate and a drunkard.' Then all the men of his town shall stone him to death." (Deut. 21:18–21a NIV). This probably horrifies our modern sensibilities. Note that the parents do not execute the boy themselves. They bring the charge. The men of the town carry out the sentence. Order was to be kept.

"'These are the LORD's appointed feasts, the sacred assemblies you are to proclaim at their appointed times: The LORD's Passover begins at twilight on the fourteenth day of the first month. On the fifteenth day of that month the LORD's Feast of Unleavened Bread begins;

for seven days you must eat bread made without yeast. On the first day hold a sacred assembly and do no regular work. For seven days present an offering made to the Lord by fire. And on the seventh day hold a sacred assembly and do no regular work.'" (Lev. 23:4–8 NIV). Have you been to a Passover or Feast of Unleavened Bread lately? No? Why not? It is commanded!

"You must therefore make a distinction between clean and unclean animals and between unclean and clean birds. Do not defile yourselves by any animal or bird or anything that moves along the ground—those which I have set apart as unclean for you. You are to be holy to me because I, the Lord, am holy, and I have set you apart from the nations to be my own." (Lev. 20:25–26 NIV). Do you eat kosher foods? That is what this commandment requires.

Peter had kept these kosher dietary laws from his birth. But then *God changed the rules*. Look at the account.

I was in the city of Joppa praying, and in a trance I saw a vision. I saw something like a large sheet being let down from heaven by its four corners, and it came down to where I was. I looked into it and saw four-footed animals of the earth, wild beasts, reptiles, and birds of the air. Then I heard a voice telling me, "Get up, Peter. Kill and eat." ¶ I replied, "Surely not, Lord! Nothing impure or unclean has ever entered my mouth." ¶ The voice spoke from heaven a second time, "Do not call anything impure that God has made clean." This happened three times, and then it was all pulled up to heaven again. (Acts 11:5–10 NIV).

What was God saying to Peter? He was telling Peter that he was *changing the rules*! The Old Testament rules no longer applied. God had a new plan. Peter had kept rigidly to kosher food and other laws for his entire life, so this change had to be very difficult for him. But the Holy Spirit changed his mind. He said, "So if God gave them the same gift as he gave us, who believed in the Lord Jesus Christ, who was I to think that I could oppose God?" (Acts 11:17 NIV).

After this, Peter went with the Gentiles (gasp!) and even entered their houses—something Peter would never have done before the vision. Later we see Peter ministering even to Greeks. The disciples now understood clearly that the gospel was for the world, not just for the Hebrews.

That is really earthshaking. Is there any other indication of God changing his approach to humanity? Consider these words of Jesus: "Do not think that I have come to abolish the Law or the Prophets; I have not come to abolish them but *to fulfill* them." (Matt. 5:17 NIV, emphasis added). "No, I came *to accomplish their purpose.*" (Matt. 5:17 NLT, emphasis added). "I'm not here to demolish but *to complete.*" (Matt. 5:17b MSG, emphasis added).

"Fulfillment" certainly looked like change to the people of Jesus' day. From our perspective, we can see it as completing God's plan.

Let me show you another passage. Paul said that *the Law is no longer in effect for us.* (However, the moral law of the Ten Commandments still tells us God's nature. Paul's use of the word *law* applied to the first five books of our Bible.)

"But before faith came, we were kept under the law, shut up unto the faith which should afterwards be revealed. Wherefore the law was our schoolmaster to bring us unto Christ, that we might be justified by faith. But after that faith is come, we are *no longer under a schoolmaster.*" (Gal. 3:23–25 KJV, emphasis added). "Now that faith has come, we are *no longer under the supervision of the law.*" (Gal. 3:25 NIV, emphasis added).

Jesus had come and presented a new and better way.

The old priesthood of Aaron perpetuated itself automatically, father to son, without explicit confirmation by God. But then God intervened and called this new, permanent priesthood into being with an added promise: God gave his word; he won't take it back: 'You're the permanent priest.'¶ *This makes Jesus the guarantee of a far better way between us and God—one that really works! A new covenant.* (Heb. 7:20–22 MSG, emphasis added).

Now Jesus dropped a bombshell: a new commandment! There were already 613 commandments in the laws of Moses. Jesus made number 614. Clearly this trumped all that had gone before. *"A new command* I give you: Love one another. As I have loved you, so you must love one another. By this all men will know that you are my disciples, if you love one another" (John 13:34–35 NIV, emphasis added).

The way of love is clearly the path that the followers of Jesus are to take.

Are we all apostles? Are we all prophets? Are we all teachers? Do we all have the power to do miracles? Do we all have the gift of healing? Do we all have the ability to speak in unknown languages? Do we all have the ability to interpret unknown languages? Of course not! So you should earnestly desire the most helpful gifts.¶ But now let me show you a way of life that is best of all.¶ If I could speak all the languages of earth and of angels, but didn't love others, I would only be a noisy gong or a clanging cymbal. If I had the gift of prophecy, and if I understood all of God's secret plans and possessed all knowledge, and if I had such faith that I could move mountains, but didn't love others, I would be nothing. If I gave everything I have to the poor and even sacrificed my body, I could boast about it; but if I didn't love others, I would have gained nothing.¶ Love is patient and kind. Love is not jealous or boastful or proud or rude. It does not demand its own way. It is not irritable, and it keeps no record of being wronged. It does not rejoice about injustice but rejoices whenever the truth wins out. Love never gives up, never loses faith, is always hopeful, and endures through every circumstance.¶ Prophecy and speaking in unknown languages and special knowledge will become useless. But love will last forever! Now our knowledge is partial and incomplete, and even the gift of prophecy reveals only part of the whole picture! But when full understanding comes, these partial things will become useless.¶ When I was a child, I spoke and thought and reasoned as a child. But when I grew up, I put away childish things. Now we see things imperfectly as in a cloudy mirror, but then we will see everything with perfect clarity. All that I know now is partial and incomplete, but then I will know everything completely, just as God now knows me completely.¶ Three things will last forever—faith, hope, and love—and the greatest of these is love. (1 Cor. 12:29–31; 13:1–13 NLT).

Within the Bible there is a progression of God's revealing of himself. The Old Testament is the foundation; it shows the holiness of God in judgment. But the Old Testament has been fulfilled, completed in Jesus. His new way is the way of love.

No, all parts of the Bible do not apply to us now. The sacrifice system of the Old Testament is gone, because Jesus became the final, ultimate sacrifice. The civil, hygienic, and ritual laws no longer apply, because Jesus has become the fulfillment of those laws.

The Ten Commandments, however, still demonstrate the nature of God and present God's plan for our lives.

Through most of the Old Testament, God is seen as the unapproachable Creator. The Hebrews' God was far away. The brutality and immorality of these people amaze us. But there were glimpses of a wounded, divine love that was God reaching out to his people. Then, in the New Testament, the full flower of God's love is seen in Jesus Christ.

Jesus taught of the Father who yearns for the wandering son to come to his senses and come home (in the parable of the prodigal son). He reached out beyond his nation to all people. Jesus crossed the cultural barrier to recognize women as persons of dignity. Finally, He became the final sacrifice, "the Lamb of God that takes away the sin of the world." Our understanding of God moved from the unapproachable Yahweh in the Old Testament, to "Abba" or "Papa," our Father in the New Testament.

CHAPTER 34

IS THERE ANY MORE EVIDENCE OF PROGRESSION OF REVELATION?

"What do you think of those churches that make the women sit on one side and men on the other?" Jody asked. "Are they afraid we will bite?"

Phil laughed. "I think that is just a custom, but I'm not sure."

The prophets occasionally looked forward to the coming of the Promised One, the Anointed One, the Messiah. Ezekiel prophesied that a *shepherd* was coming. "For this is what the Sovereign LORD says: I myself will search for my sheep and look after them. As a shepherd looks after his scattered flock when he is with them, so will I look after my sheep. I will rescue them from all the places where they were scattered on a day of clouds and darkness." (Ezek. 34:11–12 NIV).

Jesus said clearly that he was that promised shepherd. "I am the good shepherd. The good shepherd lays down his life for the sheep." (John 10:11 NIV).

Isaiah saw a day coming when God would show the way to live. "Whether you turn to the right or to the left, your ears will hear a voice behind you, saying, 'This is *the way*; walk in it.'" (Isa. 30:21 NIV, emphasis added). "Jesus answered, '*I am the way* and the truth and the life. No one comes to the Father except through me. If you really knew me, you would know my Father as well. From now on, you do know him and have seen him.'" (John 14:6–7 NIV).

Jesus said with authority that *he* was *the way*. Even the new movement that we now call "Christian" was at first called "the Way." It was this group of "the Way" that Saul was determined to stamp out.

Saul asked "for letters to the synagogues in Damascus, so that if he found any there who belonged to *the Way*, whether men or women, he might take them as prisoners to Jerusalem." (Acts 9:2b NIV, emphasis added).

The prophet Jeremiah saw God's way as true and his nature as true, requiring truth. "Go up and down the streets of Jerusalem, look around and consider, search through her squares. If you can find but one person who deals honestly and seeks the truth, I will forgive this city. Although they say, 'As surely as the LORD lives,' still they are swearing falsely.¶ O LORD, *do not your eyes look for truth?*" (Jer. 5:1–3a NIV, emphasis added).

"Jesus answered, 'I am the way *and the truth* and the life. No one comes to the Father except through me.'" (John 14:6 NIV, emphasis added). Here, Jesus clearly declares himself as *the truth*.

Solomon wrote many wise sayings. He stressed the goodness of life. "In the way of righteousness there is *life*; along that path is immortality." (Prov. 12:28 NIV, emphasis added).

Jesus claimed that he was the *source of life*. "Jesus answered, 'I am the way and the truth and *the life*. No one comes to the Father except through me.'" (John 14:6 NIV, emphasis added).

The "I am" sayings of Jesus may seem strange to us, but they came directly from Hebrew Scriptures.

"Their vine comes from the vine of Sodom and from the fields of Gomorrah. Their grapes are filled with poison, and their clusters with bitterness. Their wine is the venom of serpents, the deadly poison of cobras." (Deut. 32:32–33 NIV). Jesus was not a poisonous vine, but a good, true one. "I am *the true vine*, and my Father is the gardener." (John 15:1 NIV, emphasis added).

Old Testament writers wrote of the bread of angels, the bread of tears and wickedness, the bread of idleness and affliction, and the bread of mourners. This referred to the things people "feed" on. Jesus was saying, "Feed on *me*." "Then Jesus declared, 'I am the bread of life.'" (John 6:35a NIV). "At this the Jews began to grumble about him because he said, 'I am the bread that came down from heaven.'" (John 6:41 NIV).

All of us have heard this passage read during the Christmas season. It prophesied the coming of Jesus as the Light of the World. "The people walking in darkness have seen *a great light*; on those living in the land of the shadow of death a light has dawned." (Isa. 9:2 NIV, emphasis added).

Jesus clearly claimed that title for himself. He was *the Light*. "When Jesus spoke again to the people, he said, 'I am *the light of the world*.

Whoever follows me will never walk in darkness, but will have the light of life.'" (John 8:12 NIV, emphasis added).

Probably all of us remember singing "Jacob's Ladder" in Sunday school. This is a children's song about Jacob's dream in which he saw angels coming and going to and from heaven. Jacob felt that this place was the gate to heaven. "He was afraid and said, 'How awesome is this place! This is none other than the house of God; this is *the gate of heaven.*" (Gen. 28:17 NIV, emphasis added).

The Psalms also refer to the "gate of the Lord." "Open for me the gates of righteousness; I will enter and give thanks to the LORD. This is *the gate of the LORD* through which the righteous may enter." (Ps. 118:19–20 NIV, emphasis added).

But Jesus made this personal. He claimed it for himself. He was *the gate.* "Therefore Jesus said again, 'I tell you the truth, *I am the gate* for the sheep. All who ever came before me were thieves and robbers, but the sheep did not listen to them.'" (John 10:7–8 NIV, emphasis added).

There are many illustrations of the progression of revelation. Dallas Willard said: "The story of the New Testament is the story of the people's increasing understanding of who Jesus was."[1]

At the beginning of the New Testament, the people saw Jesus as a rabbi/teacher/prophet. Late in Jesus' ministry, Peter came to see him as the promised Messiah, but in Hebrew minds, this was still an earthly figure. However, by the end of the New Testament, the early church came to recognize Jesus as God, the Son, the cosmic King of the new creation.

"Out of his mouth comes a sharp sword with which to strike down the nations. 'He will rule them with an iron scepter.' He treads the winepress of the fury of the wrath of God Almighty. On his robe and on his thigh he has this name written: 'KING OF KINGS AND LORD OF LORDS.'" (Rev. 19:15–16 NIV).

What we must see in all of these pictures is that God did not reveal all of himself at once. Across many years, in the lives of many people, God revealed a bit more of himself. Throughout the Bible, the believers knew that a promised Anointed One, the Messiah, was coming. And we see in the passages above that they all were fulfilled in Jesus. He is the goal, the completion of God's plan.

The revelation of God moves from a faraway, fearsome God to the friend of sinners in the completed kingdom. That is a marvelous progression of his self-revelation!

Certainly, if God had told Abraham all that we know now, he would not have been able to process it. Sometimes it boggles our minds.

Let's go back to Jody's question: do all of these Old Testament laws apply to us now? No. Peter went to Jerusalem to confer with the leaders about the new converts who were not Hebrew, asking if these converts should be bound by Old Testament laws. Their decision was this: "In asking you to do this, we're not going back on our agreement regarding Gentiles who have become believers. We continue to hold fast to what we wrote in that letter, namely, to be careful not to get involved in activities connected with idols; to avoid serving food offensive to Jewish Christians; to guard the morality of sex and marriage." (Acts 21:25 MSG).

Jesus is the fulfillment, the goal of the Old Testament laws. Don't get caught up in laws that no longer apply to us. Focus on Jesus. Live the "Jesus way."

CHAPTER 35

ARE ALL PARTS OF THE BIBLE INTERCHANGEABLE?

"I don't understand why people would go back to difficult parts of the law if Jesus is the law's fulfillment," Phil stressed.

"Maybe they think all parts of the Bible are still equal," suggested Jody.

The Bible does contain many different parts. They are written in many different styles by numerous authors. Usually their purposes were different. But the unifying feature is this: *each writer was always showing God's touch on their lives*. We need to look for God within each part. But notice how they vary.

Early history: This material was all brought to us by storytelling through many generations. Before writing was readily available, it was the only option. This is found in Genesis 1–11. Theologically, this material is very important. It establishes God's relationship to humanity. We are not an accident; we were created for fellowship with God!

Pedigree: The family tree of many players in the Bible was extremely important to them and their descendants. They needed to prove they were in line to receive the covenants of God. These are found in Genesis 10, Genesis 35, Genesis 46, Exodus 1, 1 Chronicles 9, Nehemiah 7, Ruth 4, Matthew 1, etc.

The story of the Hebrews: Beginning with Abraham, this material was carefully written. They used a calendar different from ours, but any Hebrew scholar knows *exactly* when things happened. This was always written from God's point-of-view. These are the history books, beginning with the later parts of Genesis through 2 Chronicles.

Wise sayings: This is the collected wisdom of Israel, primarily from King Solomon. These are found in Proverbs, Ecclesiastes, etc.

Song words: The words of the hymns of Hebrew worship are found in the book of Psalms. Many people today find their spirits touched mightily by these lyrics.

Erotic material: This is found in the Song of Solomon. Our sexual nature is God's design and creation. The Hebrews gave praise to God for all blessings. Sexual attraction and fulfillment is certainly one of them. They did not have the Puritan hang-ups of present-day Christianity! Today many interpreters spiritualize this material to make it refer to Christ's love for the church.

Messages of warning: The prophets warned Israel about neglecting God—and impending judgment if they did not turn back to God. This material also contained flashes of future events. These are the prophets from Isaiah to Malachi.

The life of Jesus: We have four different viewpoints of Jesus' life. Mark, Matthew, and Luke are very Hebrew, and John is very Greek. These are universally called the Gospels, "the good news" of God coming to humanity in Jesus Christ.

Baby steps of the church: There was explosive new growth in the church. Then the new believers were scattered over the known world. This account is found in Acts (formerly called the Acts of the Apostles).

Correcting problems in the church: Human nature reared its ugly head within the fellowship and had to be corrected. This is found in the writings from Romans through James.

Dangers to the church: Outside challenges threatened to dilute or reshape the message. Related writings are near the end of the Bible: 1 Peter through Jude.

Visions of the end: These scenes are painted in broad strokes, using the symbols of the Old Testament. Evil is shown receiving judgment. Jesus is presented as the cosmic King. These visions are found in portions of Daniel, Ezekiel, Isaiah, and Revelation.

Are these parts or writing styles listed above interchangeable? Absolutely not!

Yes, "a rose is a rose is a rose is a rose!" But pedigree is not proverbs, and proverbs are not visions of the end. Each type of material must be read in its own style and understood through its own filter. To try to force each of these types of material into the same mold is to violate their purpose!

We should never pick passages out of context and mix them. To take a phrase out of a proverb and mix it with a piece of a vision produces this terrible message:

"The fear of the LORD is the beginning of knowledge," (Prov. 1:7a NIV). "He deceived the inhabitants of the earth." (Rev. 13:14b NIV).

Our preachers and teachers have a wealth of information in the Bible to work from. It is the thrilling account of God coming to meet human need. There is no need to mangle the accounts in the Bible to create an interesting message. This out-of-context mixing of types of literature creates confusion and can create a false message! And mixing types of literature violates the rules of language!

Each type of literature in the Bible tells, in its own way, of one great God.

CHAPTER 36

WHERE CAN I FIND CERTAIN PEOPLE IN THE BIBLE?

"Can you remember where the story of Elijah is?" Jody asked. "There isn't any book of Elijah."

"No." Phil grinned. "And there isn't any book of David or Hezekiah either."

I can help you find some of the major Bible figures.

Moses is probably the first one you may want to know about. The account of Moses begins in Exodus, the second book of the Bible. There are 295 references to Moses in Exodus. This book is the heart of the Old Testament. It tells of God using Moses to save his people from the terrible bondage of slavery. You will find hundreds more references to Moses in the next three books where the laws are listed. His death is mentioned in Deuteronomy 34.

Elijah was the greatest prophet. Moses, the great law-giver, and Elijah, the great prophet, met with Jesus at the transfiguration. You will find Elijah beginning in 1 Kings 17. We are not told of his birth; he just suddenly appears in the record. His contest with the prophets of Baal is in 1 Kings 18. The vineyard struggle against Jezebel is in 1 Kings 21. Elijah is caught up to heaven without dying in 2 Kings 2.

Jonah was the prophet who did not want his enemies to repent. He knew God well enough to know that if they repented, they would be forgiven, and he did not want them to be forgiven. He wanted God to destroy them. (This sounds like us sometimes, doesn't it?) His story is found in the little book of Jonah, only four chapters long. This is one of the earliest records of God's love for people who were not descendants of Abraham.

Hosea was the prophet who married a prostitute (unheard of). He did so at God's command, to illustrate that God still loved Israel, even though the nation had broken their covenant relationship with him. God was still trying to call them back to himself. Hosea's story is found in the little book bearing his name.

Isaiah contains some of the most beautiful and powerful language ever written. This book naturally falls into two sections: chapters 1 through 39, and 40 through 66. Be sure to read chapters 6, 40, and 53. Isaiah is in the book that carries his own name. *Nelson's Bible Dictionary* says: "The Book of Isaiah presents more insights into the nature of God than any other book of the Old Testament."[1]

Daniel is about much more than the lion's den. Daniel is the Old Testament book about the kingdom of God. Here, the phrase "Son of Man" is defined in Daniel 7:13–14. Daniel is found in the book that bears his own name. Be sure to read this before Revelation.

"Ezekiel saw the wheel, way up in the middle of the air." We all know the song better than the book. Ezekiel saw fantastic visions that are

often echoed in Revelation. Read this before reading Revelation. Ezekiel's book carries his own name.

Jeremiah was known as the weeping prophet, because he saw the destruction of Jerusalem coming. He tried to call the people to repentance, often by acting out some picture of desperate need. His book carries his name.

King David is found all over the Old Testament. His contributions are numerous. The people knew him as a great warrior king who gave them a stable, prosperous life. *Nelson's Illustrated Bible Dictionary* says: "[DAY vid] (*beloved*)—second king of the United Kingdom of the Hebrew people, ancestor of Jesus Christ, and writer of numerous psalms. The record of David's life is found in 1 Samuel 19–31; 2 Samuel 1–24; 1 Kings 1–2; and 1 Chronicles 10–29."[2]

King Solomon was David's son. He built the temple and was the collector of wisdom in books known as Proverbs, Ecclesiastes, and Song of Solomon. He reigned over Israel's most prosperous time. His birth is found in 2 Samuel 12, and his life is in 1 Kings. His death is listed in 1 Kings 11:43. Almost 250 references to his name are found in the Bible.

Jesus, of course, is found in the four Gospels: Matthew, Mark, Luke, and John.

Obviously, this kind of listing could go on and on. My purpose here is to help you find some of the best-known personalities of the Bible.

CHAPTER 37

WHICH TRANSLATION IS BEST?

"Phil, I am puzzled about this verse," said Jody. "It says in 1 Thessalonians 4:15 that 'we which are alive and remain unto the coming of the Lord shall not prevent them which are asleep.' What are we going to prevent? That doesn't make sense to me."

"I don't get it either," said Phil. "Let's check another translation."

The problem is that Jody is reading the King James Version, a translation that is four hundred years old. Since that time, some words have changed their meanings. *Prevent* is one of them. It used to mean "precede." Now it means "to stop an action."

While preparing this manuscript, I was working in a local nursing home. I shared with several of my coworkers what I was writing about. Two of them immediately asked, "Are you using the King James Version?" I knew both of these individuals to be wonderful people who lived out their faith in Christ. Obviously, they had been under the teaching of a pastor who felt that the King James translation was the best or only accurate translation.

The King James Version of 1611 was a marvelous translation in that day. The translators spared no effort to make an accurate and beautiful Bible that could be read by the masses. *National Geographic* magazine said this about it:

The King James Bible has sewn itself into the fabric of the language. If a child is ever the apple of her parent's eye or an idea seems as old as the hills, if we are at death's door or our wits end, if we have gone through a baptism of fire or are about to bite the dust, if it seems at times that the blind are leading the blind, or we are casting pearls before swine, if you are either buttering someone up or casting the first stone, the King James Bible, whether we know it or not, is speaking through us.[1]

This translation, as no other, has affected our language. It is beautiful, majestic English. What is not generally known is that there have been frequent updates of the 1611 format. These have been required to keep up with the changes in the language of the readers. Until the most recent update, which is called the New King James Version, many readers of today were struggling with outdated usage.

Since the translation of the King James Version in 1611, many archeological findings have advanced our understanding of ancient languages. Large deposits of ancient material have been found that show how particular words were used in everyday commerce. The translators of 1611 did the best they could with what was available then. Today we have much more data, and therefore we need to update the translation.

It will come as a surprise to some that the Bible was *not* written in their native English language. Many seem to think that King James' English was the original language of the Bible. But no! The Old Testament was written in Hebrew. The New Testament was written in Koine ("street" or common) Greek. And there are smatterings of

Aramaic (a language from Canaan, north of Israel, but related to Hebrew). So, unless you are a Hebrew/Greek scholar, you will need a translation.

Today there are so many!

> Bible in Basic English
> Complete Jewish Bible
> Darby Bible
> Douay Bible
> English Standard Version
> God's Word Translation
> Jerusalem Bible
> King James Version
> New American Standard Bible
> New International Version
> New King James Version
> New Living Translation
> New World Translation
> Revised Standard Version
> New Revised Standard Version
> The Amplified Bible
> The Living Bible
> The Message
> Today's English Version
> Young's Literal Translation

And these are only *some* of the translations available today! There are fifty-plus translations available to readers of English. But which one is the perfect translation?

R.C. Sproul wrote: "As New Testament professor D. A. Carson says, 'No translation is perfect.'"[2] There cannot *be* a perfect one! Why not?

When we go from one language to another, we do find equivalent words that will translate well. Usually they are names for concrete things, such as *door, window, bed, house*, and similar items.

But we also find many abstract words that have *no equivalent word* in the other language. An illustration from the Bible is found in John 14:16. The word used there to describe the Holy Spirit is *"parakleton"* (*John 14:16,* παράκλετον in Greek), which has no exact equivalent in English. Look how the various translators handle it.

> "And he will give you another *Counselor…*" (John 14:16b NIV).

> "And he will give you another *Advocate,*" (John 14:16b NLT).

> "And he'll provide you another *Friend…*" (John 14:16b MSG).

> "And He will give you another *Helper,*" (John 14:16b NASB).

> "And He will give you another *Comforter (Counselor, Helper, Intercessor, Advocate, Strengthener, and Standby),*" (John 14:16b AB).

The word *parakleton* has such big meanings in the original Greek that we have to use a series of words to translate it well into English. Most translators are very concerned about making the text too long, so they settle for a word that is partly or nearly correct. They try to get as close to the meaning as they can, but that attempt is never exact, never perfect. And there are many words for *ideas* or *concepts* that have no exact equivalent in another language.

Another problem is that the word order differs when we go from one language to another. A humorous illustration we have all seen is from the Pennsylvania Dutch: "Throw the horse over the fence some hay!" That is perfect word order for German. But when the same word order is maintained in English, we find it odd or funny. A direct word-for-word translation from Greek to English is very choppy, very difficult to understand.

A word-for-word reading of the familiar John 3:16 from *Young's Literal Translation* goes like this: "For God did so love the world, that His Son—the only begotten—He gave, that every one who is believing in him may not perish, but may have life age-during." (John 3:16 YLT).

The *New International Version* reads: "For God so loved the world that he gave his one and only Son, that whoever believes in him shall not perish but have eternal life." (John 3:16 NIV).

Word order often *must* be changed to make the thought understandable in another language. In some situations, the scholars differ in the word order they select, so again, the translation cannot be perfect.

Another potential problem is *translator bias.* An honest translator tries to be objective, but when faced with an obscure passage, the meaning of which is not readily obvious, the translator naturally chooses words that make sense to him or her. In situations like this, the translator's theology naturally comes into play, and a theological bias is shown.

An illustration of this is found in Matthew 11:12 in the literal translation by Young: "And, from the days of John the Baptist till now, the reign of the heavens doth suffer violence, and violent men do take it by force," (Matt. 11:12 YLT).

The King James Version says, "And from the days of John the Baptist until now the kingdom of heaven suffereth violence, and the violent take it by force." (Matt. 11:12 KJV). This meaning agrees with Young's translation above. But look at the next one.

"From the days of John the Baptist until now, the kingdom of heaven has been forcefully advancing, and forceful men lay hold of it." (Matt. 11:12 NIV). This translation stresses that the *kingdom is advancing* with power.

"And from the time John the Baptist began preaching until now, the Kingdom of Heaven has been forcefully advancing, and violent people are attacking it." (Matt. 11:12 NLT). This one has the kingdom advancing powerfully but *being attacked* by opponents.

"For a long time now people have tried to force themselves into God's kingdom." (Matt. 11:12 MSG). This one stresses that *people are forcing themselves into the kingdom.*

The different meanings are easily seen, especially in the last three translations. Obviously, the translators are not sure what this passage means and are trying to make sense of it.

Still another difficulty was explained in chapter 24. All native speakers use idioms, such as "by the skin of his teeth" or "butterflies in my stomach." The Hebrew and Greek idioms are not always well understood, *nor are they always correctly translated.*

So, let's change the question. "Which is the *best* translation?" The answer will depend on the answer to this question: "Best for what?" If you want to do a word study (looking at the shades of meaning in one word), one of the best translations is the *New American Standard Bible* (NASB). The translators have tried to be as accurate as possible to the original words and word order. Though accurate, this translation is "choppy," not easy reading.

If you want beautiful English, go to the *King James Version* (KJV) or the *New King James Version* (NKJV), which updates many outmoded words and improves word order.

If you want accuracy with better flowing English, try the *New International Version* (NIV).

If you are willing to sacrifice word accuracy for very easy-to-understand street English, try *The Message* (MSG) or the *New Living Translation* (NLT). Note the examples below that compare 1 Corinthians 13:9–12 in the NASB, NIV, NLT, and MSG.

For we know in part, and we prophesy in part; but when the perfect comes, the partial will be done away. When I was a child, I used to speak as a child, think as a child, reason as a child; when I became a man, I did away with childish things. For now we see in a mirror dimly, but then face to face; now I know in part, but then I shall know fully just as I also have been fully known. (1 Cor. 13:9–12 NASB).

For we know in part and we prophesy in part, but when perfection comes, the imperfect disappears. When I was a child, I talked like a child, I thought like a child, I reasoned like a child. When I became a man, I put childish ways behind me. Now we see but a poor reflection as in a mirror; then we shall see face to face. Now I know in part; then I shall know fully, even as I am fully known. (1 Cor. 13:9–12 NIV).

Now our knowledge is partial and incomplete, and even the gift of prophecy reveals only part of the whole picture! But when full understanding comes, these partial things will become useless.¶

When I was a child, I spoke and thought and reasoned as a child. But when I grew up, I put away childish things. Now we see things imperfectly as in a cloudy mirror, but then we will see everything with perfect clarity. All that I know now is partial and incomplete, but then I will know everything completely, just as God now knows me completely. (1 Cor. 13:9-12 NLT).

We know only a portion of the truth, and what we say about God is always incomplete. But when the Complete arrives, our incompletes will be canceled.¶ When I was an infant at my mother's breast, I gurgled and cooed like any infant. When I grew up, I left those infant ways for good.¶ We don't yet see things clearly. We're squinting in a fog, peering through a mist. But it won't be long before the weather clears and the sun shines bright! We'll see it all then, see it all as clearly as God sees us, knowing him directly just as he knows us! (1 Cor. 13:9-12 MSG).

I strongly recommend using *multiple versions*. One version may leave you wondering about the meaning, but checking that same passage in several versions will usually clear it up for you. To fill this need, many publishers have printed parallel Bibles and/or parallel New Testaments. These often list the King James Version first, then the New American Standard, and then two other new translations or paraphrases. (A paraphrase is not accurate word-for-word, but it tries to put the idea of the whole passage into current English.) You can read straight across the two pages and see the same verse in four translations. After reading the four translations, most people understand it. Keep in mind that parallel Bibles are four books in one, so they are quite large. Even a parallel New Testament is a large book.

A number of publishing companies have created study Bibles. These have explanations in the center column, side columns, or in prefaces or footnotes. They also usually have a small Bible dictionary and atlas in the back. These supports can be very helpful, but be aware that the material they add *is not Scripture.* It is someone's interpretation, readily allowing their theological bias to be presented.

Rapidly expanding technology includes devices like the smartphone, iPad, Nook, Kindle, etc. Take a look at the *Wave Study Bible* on Google for more information. When I last looked, they were offering eight different translations for comparison on your electronic device.

I'd like to make another strong suggestion. Always read the foreword, preface, and introduction of any Bible. In it you will find the goals used for the translation, and the names of the translators or editorial board. Any intellectually honest translator or group will take credit for their lifetime of work and will be willing to defend their work to other scholars.

In contrast, there are groups that start with their own sets of beliefs (theology) and then add, subtract, or change words in their Bible to make the Bible fit what they believe. They change the Bible, bending it to their purposes! This is intellectually dishonest and cannot be supported by real Hebrew/Greek scholars. These so-called translations, not surprisingly, do not list the translators. Followers of these movements are taught that their translation is the only one that is correct and that they are to avoid all others. Avoid such intellectually dishonest versions.

In summary, no translation can be perfect. Use several versions to grasp difficult-to-understand passages. Above all, avoid translations that leave you puzzled.

From the Holy Spirit to print to our spirits, God still speaks to us today!

CHAPTER 38

WHAT IS THE BIBLE ALL ABOUT?

"I just had a friend ask me what the Bible is all about," Jody said. "I know it's about Jesus, David, Paul—but I just didn't know how to answer her."

"What you said is right," Phil responded, "but for me that doesn't say it all."

Summarizing an anthology is difficult, but we should be able to place the Bible in a category and tell what it does there.

The Bible is about God and how he relates to us. The Bible is a spiritual book that tells how God came to us through the fathers (patriarchs), the prophets, and finally through Jesus.

The story is told of a farmer in Grandpa's day who simply could not understand why God would come to earth in Jesus. One bitterly cold, blustery winter day, he saw a flock of birds in the large apple tree just behind the barn. *They'll freeze tonight*, he thought. *I'll open the large barn doors and let them come into the hay mow for shelter.* He opened the door and backed away to watch.

None came in. So he tried to chase them in. They flew about, but not one entered the barn. Then he tried to attract them with some grain scattered near the door and inside. They took the grain but quickly flew back to the apple tree. *How can I get them to do what is good for them? If only I were a bird, I could lead them in to safety.*

And in a flash of insight, he suddenly understood why Jesus had come to earth.

The central message of the Bible is that *God has always been involved with his creation.* At first, it was through intimate fellowship. Then, after Adam and Eve rebelled against God, there was separation. God called humanity to come to him, and a few did. Noah obeyed God. Abraham obeyed God. The prophets obeyed him. Finally, God came to us in human form to save us. He came as an innocent baby, born into a poor family over in Israel.

Many people ask, "Wasn't Jesus just a man from Nazareth?" The Bible says that Jesus had a divine birth. It says that he was born of a virgin. "This is how the birth of Jesus Christ came about: His mother Mary was pledged to be married to Joseph, but before they came together, she was found to be with child through the Holy Spirit." (Matt. 1:18 NIV).

With humanity, it just doesn't work that way! Reproduction takes a male and a female. The virgin birth is a claim of divinity. Jesus was much more than a man.

Yes, there were others at that time who claimed to be the product of a virgin birth. The Caesars did so as a way of unifying their political power over their people. But nothing else in their lives convinces us today that their statement was true.

In addition to the claim of a virgin birth, we have the explicit claims of Jesus. He taught both in *words* and in *actions*.

Let's start with his words. "I tell you the truth," Jesus answered, "before Abraham was born, I am!" (John 8:58 NIV). The average reader today is probably confused by these words of Jesus. It is clear to us that Abraham lived many years before Jesus was born, so what does Jesus mean by "I am"?

We need to understand what every Hebrew knew to his core: *the name of God.* For that understanding, we need to go back in the Old Testament to the place where God called Moses to lead the Hebrew people out of slavery. "Moses said to God, 'Suppose I go to the Israelites and say to them, "The God of your fathers has sent me to you," and they ask me, "What is his name?" Then what shall I tell them?'¶ God said to Moses, 'I AM WHO I AM. This is what you are to say to the Israelites: "I AM has sent me to you."'" (Ex. 3:13–14 NIV).

Throughout the entire Bible, the premier name of God is "I Am." Commentators have written extensively on its meaning. It certainly means that God is saying that he is self-existent, that he is real— more real than anything else. The name *Yahweh* (in Hebrew) and *Jehovah* (in English) are forms of this title, "I Am."

In claiming this title for himself, Jesus was saying that he is God! God's premier name is "I Am" and Jesus called himself "I Am." Since he was obviously a human being standing in the presence of other human beings, they felt that this was an extreme insult, or blasphemy, to the eternal Creator God, and they tried unsuccessfully to kill him on the spot.

Next, we need to look at the series of "I am" sayings of Jesus. These are found in the gospel of John.

"Then Jesus declared, '*I am* the bread of life. He who comes to me will never go hungry, and he who believes in me will never be thirsty.'" (John 6:35 NIV).

"When Jesus spoke again to the people, he said, '*I am* the light of the world. Whoever follows me will never walk in darkness, but will have the light of life.'" (John 8:12 NIV).

"*I am* the gate; whoever enters through me will be saved." (John 10:9 NIV).

"*I am* the good shepherd. The good shepherd lays down his life for the sheep." (John 10:11 NIV).

"Why then do you accuse me of blasphemy because I said, '*I am* God's Son'? Do not believe me unless I do what my Father does." (John 10:36–37 NIV).

"Jesus said to her, '*I am* the resurrection and the life. He who believes in me will live, even though he dies; and whoever lives and believes in me will never die.'" (John 11:25–26 NIV).

"I am telling you now before it happens, so that when it does happen you will believe that *I am* He." (John 13:19 NIV).

"Jesus answered, '*I am* the way and the truth and the life. No one comes to the Father except through me.'" (John 14:6 NIV).

"*I am* the true vine, and my Father is the gardener." (John 15:1 NIV).

All of these titles are associated with God in the Old Testament. The casual Greek/Western reader might miss the connection, but a

Hebrew reader would be absolutely certain that Jesus meant to say that he *was* and *is* God.

Seen as a unit, these titles that Jesus claims for himself are astounding! Was he crazy or a liar, or was he speaking truth? The church has always affirmed that he was speaking truth!

Only once in the Gospels did Jesus call himself "the Son of God." "I tell you the truth, a time is coming and has now come when the dead will hear the voice of the *Son of God* and those who hear will live." (John 5:25 NIV).

Twice Jesus referred to himself as "God's Son." "Why then do you accuse me of blasphemy because I said, 'I am *God's Son*'?" (John 10:36 NIV). "When he heard this, Jesus said, 'This sickness will not end in death. No, it is for God's glory so that *God's Son* may be glorified through it.'" (John 11:4 NIV).

We understand that the titles "Son of God" and "God's Son" that Jesus used to refer to himself are divine titles. Others regularly used them to refer to Jesus. "But these are written that you may believe that *Jesus is the Christ, the Son of God*." (John 20:31 NIV). "At once he began to preach in the synagogues that *Jesus is the Son of God*." (Acts 9:20 NIV).

The next title we need to consider is "Son of Man." Many have said that Jesus was identifying with humanity by using that title, but this is an attempt to use our Greek/Western way of looking at the world to understand it. Such an explanation is far from the truth. The *Dictionary of Biblical Imagery* says, "Son of Man is not a counterweight to Son of God, as if each points to a different side of Christ's nature—the human and the divine."[1] To think this way is to allow our Greek training to look for opposites, which in this case overpowers the evidence of the Bible.

Here is a clear example of our Greek way of thinking causing a misunderstanding.

Every time Jesus called himself the "Son of Man," he was referring to the prophecy of Daniel. "In my vision at night I looked, and there before me was one like a *son of man*, coming with the clouds of heaven. He approached the Ancient of Days and was led into his presence. He was given authority, glory and sovereign power; all peoples, nations and men of every language worshiped him. His dominion is an everlasting dominion that will not pass away, and his kingdom is one that will never be destroyed." (Dan. 7:13–14 NIV).

Every time Jesus called himself the "Son of Man," he was saying that he had come from heaven, from the presence of the eternal God, by the authority of the Father, to establish the kingdom of God on earth. He was saying that he was to be worshipped! Jesus called himself "Son of Man" more than anything else. It is clearly a divine title, stressing *divinity, not humanity.*

Let's look briefly at things Jesus *did* that only God can do.

Jesus taught that the miracles he regularly performed had a greater purpose than simply relieving suffering. The miracles were proof of who he was! "Why then do you accuse me of blasphemy because I said, 'I am God's Son'? Do not believe me unless I do what my Father does. But if I do it, even though you do not believe me, *believe the miracles, that you may know and understand that the Father is in me, and I in the Father.'*" (John 10:36–38 NIV).

Jesus offered not only miracles but forgiveness. "Knowing their thoughts, Jesus said, 'Why do you entertain evil thoughts in your hearts? Which is easier: to say, "Your sins are forgiven," or to say, "Get up and walk"? But *I want you to know that the Son of Man has authority on earth to forgive sins.* Then he said to the paralytic, 'Get up, take your mat and go home.' And the man got up and went home." (Matt. 9:4–7 NIV).

Forgiveness is internal and difficult to verify, but to see a crippled man get up and walk is proof that Jesus could do what he said. And the Pharisees were right in saying that *only God* could forgive sins!

Near the end of Jesus' ministry, after the resurrection, the disciples worshipped Jesus. "Then the eleven disciples went to Galilee, to the mountain where Jesus had told them to go. When they saw him, they worshiped him; but some doubted. Then Jesus came to them and said, 'All authority in heaven and on earth has been given to me. Therefore go and make disciples of all nations,'" (Matt. 28:16–19a NIV).

The disciples, being good Hebrews, knew that they should worship *only* God (the first commandment), and they worshipped Jesus!

Next, notice Jesus' statement: "All authority in heaven and on earth has been given unto me." Again, *only God* has all authority.

The skeptics will say that these are just idle words of an egomaniac. The believer will point out that Jesus offered much more than words—his life, his ministry to the needy, his sacrificial death, and his resurrection. A liar cannot back up his words.

Further, only God can unfailingly see the future. Jesus repeatedly predicted that he would be killed and then raised back to life. When the resurrection occurred, the disciples were as confused as everyone else. Resurrection just doesn't happen to a person—unless God chooses to overrule his natural laws.

Skeptics will say that they do not believe the resurrection really happened. "Dead people simply do not come back to life. It is all a fairy tale!"

But I challenge every skeptic to explain what happened to the disciples. They were sure that Jesus was the Messiah, but they misunderstood what *kind* of rule he would bring. They were sure that he would liberate them from the Roman occupation and return the nation to their glory days. When he died on that Roman cross, they were devastated.

"What things," he asked. "About Jesus of Nazareth," they replied. "He was a prophet, powerful in word and deed before God and all the people. The chief priests and our rulers handed him over to be sentenced to death, and they crucified him; but we had hoped that he was the one who was going to redeem Israel." (Luke 24:19-21a NIV).

The disciples were justifiably afraid for their lives. Since the Romans had killed Jesus, wouldn't the Jews gather up the disciples next to be horribly tortured and killed?

"On the evening of that first day of the week, when the disciples were together, *with the doors locked for fear of the Jews*, Jesus came and stood among them and said, 'Peace be with you!' After he said this, he showed them his hands and side. The disciples were overjoyed when they saw the Lord." (John 20:19–20 NIV). A few days later, Peter went back to his old job, fishing on the Sea of Galilee.

And then, suddenly, this fearful band of disciples turned into a force that literally changed the history of the world. Of the eleven disciples remaining after Judas committed suicide, ten were killed for proclaiming the resurrection of Jesus. John was imprisoned and later exiled to the prison island of Patmos, where he died. The disciples *would not recant* their message. "With great power the apostles continued to testify to the resurrection of the Lord Jesus," (Acts 4:33 NIV).

To the skeptics, I repeat my challenge. If no resurrection of Jesus occurred, what happened to those eleven men that allowed them to change the world?

Finally, the early church struggled to explain the puzzle of a human being also being God. They attempted to put the concrete word pictures of the Hebrew mind into the abstract forms of the Greek/ Western world. The first statement came in the Nicean Creed, written by the Council of Nicaea in AD 325:

I believe in one God, the Father Almighty, Maker of heaven and earth, and of all things visible and invisible. ¶ And in one Lord Jesus Christ, the only-begotten Son of God, begotten of the Father before all worlds; God of God, Light of Light, very God of very God; begotten, not made, being of one substance with the Father, by whom all things were made.¶ Who, for us men for our salvation, came down from heaven, and was incarnate by the Holy Spirit of the virgin Mary, and was made man; and was crucified also for us under Pontius Pilate; He suffered and was buried; and the third day He rose again, according to the Scriptures; and ascended into heaven, and sits on the right hand of the Father; and He shall come again, with glory, to judge the quick and the dead; whose kingdom shall have no end.[2]

This creed, written by the Council of Chalcedon in AD 451, emphasized that Jesus was *both* God and man. It emphasized the divinity of Jesus.

Therefore, following the holy fathers, we all with one accord teach men to acknowledge one and the same Son, our Lord Jesus Christ, at once *complete in Godhead and complete in manhood, truly God and truly man,* consisting also of a reasonable soul and body; of one substance with the Father as regards his Godhead, and at the same time of one substance with us as regards his manhood; like us in all respects, apart from sin; as regards his Godhead, begotten of the Father before the ages, but yet as regards his manhood begotten, for us men and for our salvation, of Mary the Virgin, the God-bearer; one and the same Christ, Son, Lord, Only-begotten, recognized in two natures, without confusion, without change, without division, without separation; the distinction of natures being in no way annulled by the union, but rather the characteristics of each nature being preserved and coming together to form one person and subsistence, not as parted or separated into two persons, but one and the same Son and Only-begotten God the Word, Lord Jesus Christ; even as the prophets from earliest times spoke of him, and our Lord Jesus Christ himself taught us, and the creed of the fathers has handed down to us."[3] (emphasis added).

So, putting all of the evidence together—the virgin birth, Jesus' claims for himself, the titles he used for himself and others used for him, his ability to forgive sins, his miracles, his ability to predict his death and his resurrection—all of this is more than human. The early church did their best to put these truths into words by writing the creeds listed above. The only proper conclusion is that Jesus was who he said he was. Jesus *was* and *is* the "I Am." Jesus is God!

Jesus is the very heart of the Bible. If we do not know Jesus, it is impossible to understand the Bible. It is Jesus who has shown us the Father. He brought us both salvation and the kingdom. It is Jesus' Spirit that lives within the believer as the Holy Spirit. Take Jesus out of the Bible, and we do not have much left!

God has always been involved with his people. In Jesus we have seen the ultimate revelation of the Father.

I suggest that you read *The Case for Christ* by Lee Strobel.

CHAPTER 39

WHAT IS THE HINGE-POINT OF HISTORY?

"It seems to me that in all of life, something has to be the most important—you know, basic, the foundation," Jody said. "I wonder what it is?"

"That's a good question," responded Phil. "If you listen to the TV preachers, for some it is prophecy, and for others it is seed faith, stuff like that."

Max Lucado tells a stirring story in *No Wonder They Call Him the Savior.*[1] A friend posed a gut-wrenching question to him. "What counts? What is the bottom line?" His friend did not want smooth answers. He wanted reality.

I think of all the Bible stories I heard in Sunday school: Daniel in the lion's den; Shadrach, Meshach, and Abednego in the fiery furnace; Samson and Delilah; Saul and Goliath; the woman at the well with Jesus; Paul being shipwrecked; and so on. Do you have similar memories? Which one is most important?

Does the Bible contain what is *absolutely the most important event in human history*? I think so. Other believers think so. The New Testament clearly spells out the content of the "good news," the gospel, as most important: "Now, brothers, I want to remind you of the gospel I preached to you, which you received and on which you have taken your stand. By this gospel you are saved, if you hold firmly to the word I preached to you. Otherwise, you have believed in vain.¶ For what I received I passed on to you as of first importance: that *Christ died for our sins according to the Scriptures, that he was buried, that he was raised on the third day according to the Scriptures,*" (1 Cor. 15:1–3 NIV, emphasis added).

This is of first importance, the most important event in history: the suffering, death, and resurrection of Jesus, the Christ. You see, if Jesus is who he said he is, *this is the hinge-point of all human history.* Everything before this event was leading up to it, and everything after it is leading up to the completion of his kingdom. All of the Old Testament is prelude. Part of the New Testament continues the prelude, part of it is the critical moment—the ultimate sacrifice—and part of it is postlude.

The Julian and Gregorian calendars have divided history into BC (before Christ) and AD (Latin for *anno domini*, "the year of our Lord"). This designation of time is used worldwide by the United Nations and the Universal Postal Union.

Max Lucado said, "The apostles sparked a movement ... They preached 'Jesus Christ and Him crucified,' not for the lack of another topic, but because they couldn't exhaust this one. What unlocked the doors of the apostle's hearts? Simple. They saw Jesus. They encountered the Christ. Their sins collided with their Savior and their Savior won!"[2]

This says that our world turns on the real moment of meeting Jesus as our Savior. It's true! But let's look at it from the perspective of eternity.

Our Bible says that God (Father, Son, and Holy Spirit) created heaven and earth. At the appropriate time, Jesus left heaven to come to our sin-plagued earth on a rescue mission. He didn't come for a vacation or a diversion but to save a creation that could not save itself. He left the perfection of heaven to enter the malice of this planet. Then he suffered the scorn, slander, and lies of the very people he came to save. Finally, he deliberately walked into the worst that his nation and the Roman overlords could design—crucifixion. He took on himself the worst that our world could muster so that you and I could receive the best heaven has to offer. Ultimately, on the final day, Jesus will be the judge. His kingdom will be completed, fulfilled—with those who love him remaining in his presence forever. This view places the cross at the center of history.

What matters most? Not my job, or car, or house. Not my children's health. Not the economy of our nation or world. What matters most is our relationship with the Creator. There, at the cross, Jesus did for us what we could not do for ourselves.

Oh, the advertisers will tell us that we need the latest gadget or soap or perfume to add fulfillment to our lives. But do those things *really* bring deep meaning to our lives? Of course not! Our friends and associates will likely tell us that we need to fit in, be part of the gang—and there is something to be said for being socially aware. But do we give first place to friends, or to the Christ who paid for our ticket to heaven? Will our friends be there when the going gets tough? Jesus will be!

No event in history has such profound meaning as the sufferings of Jesus, the cross of Calvary, and his resurrection. Remember: Jesus could have gone the other way. He could have gotten lost in the crowds of the Ten Cities (Decapolis) and beyond. He could have refused to "take the cup of suffering" that he saw coming when he prayed in the garden of Gethsemane. He could have refused to become the "suffering servant" of Isaiah 53. But he chose instead to do the Father's will. He *chose* to die for you and me.

This is the love story that never grows old.

How often do we allow ourselves to reflect on what Jesus did for us? Most of us find it too painful. We would rather fill our minds with pleasant thoughts. We would rather watch the football game, go fishing or shopping, or do anything enjoyable. But the adage is true: "Joy is best understood after sorrow."

Our Roman Catholic brethren have, I believe, posted boldly in every church the "stations of the cross." Even if nothing is said during the service about Jesus' sacrifice for us, they are there as a visual reminder. The sufferings of Christ are emphasized. The Protestant focus is on the empty cross, implying the resurrection. This is the closing act and is extremely important. But without the sufferings and death of Christ, there would have been no resurrection. Without the resurrection, the sufferings and death would have been meaningless. These two are bound together in meaning.

You see, Jesus' sufferings for us are more important than the national economy, more important than space exploration, more important than the United Nations. What Jesus has done for us has affected every human being for all of history. Can you name one other event that has lifted every human being?

Catherine of Siena wrote in the 1300s: "The actions of our savior are so rich in meaning that every soul that ponders them finds in them its own share of spiritual food to nourish it and bring it to salvation."[3]

History turns on Jesus' death and resurrection. Before it is prelude. After it is postlude. The cross and resurrection is the main event.

CHAPTER 40

WHAT DOES *SALVATION* MEAN?

"Sarah asked me to define *salvation*," Jody said. "I told her about being saved. But later I thought that there is probably more to it. What do you think?"

"Well, I'm no theologian," Phil answered, "but I think you are right. Still, I don't know how to tell her any more that you did."

When I was about fifteen, my parents took the youth group from our church on a picnic/swimming outing. We gathered at a bend in the creek, well known as one of our local swimming holes. Most of the kids went swimming, but some stayed on the creek bank to tend the campfire. Dad was a good swimmer and jumped right in with us, swam out to the middle, and went down. I happened to be standing on the shore a bit later when Dalton said, "I'm worried about your dad. He hasn't come up for air."

I replied, "Nothing to worry about. Dad does that all the time. He took a big breath just before he went down. He's on the bottom, holding onto a big rock to see how long he can stay under."

Just then he surfaced and went back down. I said, "See? He just came up for more air." The next time he surfaced, he yelled, "Help!" Four of us teenagers immediately dived in to help pull him to the shore. Later he told us that he had simply blacked out. He didn't even remember calling for help. He was very sick for the next week because of the water he had taken into his lungs.

We four boys were salvation for Dad in that moment. We saved his physical life.

There are three major concepts that we must understand if we ever hope to understand the Bible. They are *salvation*, *grace*, and the *kingdom of God/heaven*. Without a good grasp of all these concepts, the Bible simply will not make sense. So let's wrestle with *salvation* first.

In the Old Testament, *salvation* referred to the nation of Israel being rescued or delivered from enemies. The national saviors at various times were Moses, Gideon, Samson, David, etc. The salvation referred to was military and political, and it kept the nation from being conquered. These individuals led the defense of their nation and saved them from defeat or annihilation.

Then, early in the New Testament, the angel told Joseph, "She [Mary] will give birth to a son, and you are to give him the name Jesus, because he will *save his people from their sins*." (Matt. 1:21 NIV, emphasis added).

Certainly Mary must have been amazed to have been chosen. But what did the angel mean by "save his people from their sins?" They already had the law of Moses and the sacrifice system.

This message from the angel caused a major shift in meaning. *Salvation* moved from meaning "national deliverance from conquest" to meaning "personal deliverance from sin." Salvation in the New

Testament deals with restoring our individual relationship with God. This is one of those pivotal moments in the Bible that changed everything.

In an earlier section of this book, we talked about the Hebrews' thinking and talking in word pictures. The subject of salvation is an excellent illustration of word pictures used to describe that restored relationship with God. I have cataloged thirty-five different pictures of the salvation relationship, and probably have missed some.

Salvation may be an overused term, but it is very descriptive. It pictures the sinner under the control of the Evil One, destined for an eternity away from God. Through faith in Jesus' sacrifice, the believer has been rescued from Satan by the Savior. "God *saved* you by his grace when you believed. And you can't take credit for this; it is a gift from God." (Eph. 2:8 NLT, emphasis added).

Rebirth means being "born again." It pictures being born a *second* time, where the birth is not physical but spiritual. This infers that we were spiritually dead. By God's creative miracle, we are made alive toward him. "In reply Jesus declared, 'I tell you the truth, no one can see the kingdom of God unless he is *born again*.'" (John 3:3 NIV, emphasis added).

Redemption paints the word picture of paying a ransom. This shows the sinner as a captive of Satan. Jesus paid the price to free the captive from Satan's bondage. "Christ *redeemed* us from that self-defeating, cursed life by absorbing it completely into himself." (Gal. 3:13a MSG, emphasis added).

Justification pictures a court in which the guilty party has been set free. How? By Jesus' payment of the penalty of the law. "And are *justified* freely by his grace through the redemption that came by Christ Jesus," (Rom. 3:24 NIV, emphasis added).

Atonement pictures the sinner receiving restoration with God. The focus here is the "at-one-ment" (atonement) achieved by Jesus' sacrifice. Jesus became the Lamb of God slain for the sins of the world that restores us. "And not only so, but we also joy in God through our Lord Jesus Christ, by whom we have now received the *atonement.*" (Rom. 5:11 KJV, emphasis added).

Reinstatement shows the wandering son returning home and being fully reinstated into the family. Reinstatement pictures the outrageous generosity of the father, after the son had wasted years and one third of the estate. "But the father said to his servants, 'Quick! Bring the best robe and put it on him. Put a ring on his finger and sandals on his feet. Bring the fattened calf and kill it. Let's have a feast and celebrate. For this son of mine *was dead and is alive again; he was lost and is found.*'" (Luke 15:22–24a NIV, emphasis added).

Regeneration pictures a dead body given new life. We were dead in sin, but we are given new life in Christ. "But according to His mercy He saved us, through the washing of *regeneration* and renewing of the Holy Spirit," (Titus 3:5b NKJV, emphasis added).

Conversion pictures a new use, a new direction. Broken pieces of tile are made into a gorgeous mosaic picture! A life has been turned from selfishness to Christ-likeness! "As they traveled through Phoenicia and Samaria, they told how the Gentiles had been *converted.*" (Acts 15:3b NIV, emphasis added).

Forgiveness is a picture of having been released from the burden of having been wronged. Now, because of Jesus' sacrifice on the cross, we can give and receive forgiveness. "This is my blood of the covenant, which is poured out for many for the *forgiveness* of sins." (Matt. 26:28 NIV, emphasis added).

Righteousness shows our crookedness being straightened to God's standard. This "right standing" is transferred to us by God. "So also through the obedience of the one man [Jesus] the many will be made *righteous.*" (Rom. 5:19b NIV, emphasis added).

Being found is a picture of a sheep that has been located after wandering away from the shepherd. At great expense, the shepherd has found and returned the sheep to the fold. "And if he *finds* it, doesn't he make far more over it than over the ninety-nine who stay put?" (Matt. 18:13–14 MSG, emphasis added).

Rescue pictures a person drowning in a swamp. He is calling for a lifeguard! "*Rescue* me from the mire, do not let me sink; deliver me from those who hate me, from the deep waters." (Ps. 69:14 NIV, emphasis added).

Children refers to the father/son relationship instead of a master/slave relationship. "So you have not received a spirit that makes you fearful slaves. Instead, you received God's Spirit when he adopted you as his own *children.*" (Rom. 8:15a NLT, emphasis added).

Heir speaks of those who will inherit the spiritual estate of the kingdom. "Now if we are children, then we are *heirs—heirs* of God and co-heirs with Christ" (Rom. 8:17a NIV, emphasis added). The *Dictionary of Biblical Imagery* says of *heirs*: "That matchless *inheritance* encourages the believer to endurance and faithfulness."[1]

Shelter pictures a violent windstorm or sandstorm, one that is life-threatening and scary! God is our Rock of Gibraltar that shelters us from the storm. "He who dwells in the *shelter* of the Most High will rest in the shadow of the Almighty.¶ I will say of the LORD, 'He is my refuge and my fortress, my God, in whom I trust.'" (Ps. 91:1–2 NIV, emphasis added).

Shepherd is the provider for the flock of sheep. He must know where to find pasture and water. He must protect against wild animals. He must be able to treat the wounded and bring back the lost. Without the shepherd, the sheep do not stand a chance! "Because the Lord is my Shepherd, I have everything I need!" (Ps. 23:1 TLB).

Substitution pictures the innocent accepting punishment that the guilty deserve. What kind of love goes to such lengths? "But he was pierced for our rebellion, crushed for our sins. He was beaten so we could be whole. He was whipped so we could be healed." (Isa. 53:5 NLT).

Permanent love contrasts the position of a family member to that of a slave who may be bought and sold. "Now a slave has no *permanent place* in the family, but a son belongs to it forever." (John 8:35 NIV, emphasis added).

Supremacy given to the humble sounds like a contradiction. We expect people to claw for position, but God's kingdom inverts many values of our world. "Therefore, whoever humbles himself like this child is the greatest in the kingdom of heaven." (Matt. 18:4 NIV).

Seat with Christ pictures Jesus seated in equal authority with the Father, and we are seated *with them* because we are "in Christ." How awesome is that? "And God raised us up with Christ and *seated us with him* in the heavenly realms in Christ Jesus," (Eph. 2:6 NIV, emphasis added). The *Dictionary of Biblical Imagery* says: "By faith and baptism 'into Christ', Christians have entered into a solidarity with the anointed one so that *what is true of Christ is true of his people*."[2] (emphasis added)

Propitiation comes from an old English word that means "to appease." In this use, Jesus' sacrifice on the cross paid the debt that none of us could pay. "And He Himself is the *propitiation* for our sins, and not for ours only but also for the whole world." (1 John 2:2 NKJV, emphasis added).

Fellowship of prayer is known and practiced in every Christian circle. We hold up to God our praise, thanks, worship—and needs. And

He responds with what is best in its proper time. "You faithfully *answer our prayers* with awesome deeds, O God our savior." (Ps. 65:5a NLT, emphasis added).

Holiness: Me? Holy? No way! But where God is, he makes everything holy. Even a building is made holy by his presence! Doesn't his Spirit live within you? "Therefore, I urge you, brothers, in view of God's mercy, to offer your bodies as living sacrifices, *holy* and pleasing to God—this is your spiritual act of worship." (Rom. 12:1 NIV, emphasis added).

Glory is the end step in God's plan of salvation. At the end of all human history, those who have accepted God's way will be given a "glorified" body, as Jesus had after the resurrection. "When he comes back, he will take these dying bodies of ours and change them into *glorious bodies* like his own," (Phil. 3:21a TLB, emphasis added).

Freedom pictures release from the slave trade, which was the norm in Jesus' day. The dream of every slave was to be given or to earn freedom. "So if the Son sets you *free*, you will be free indeed." (John 8:36 NIV, emphasis added).

Illumination allows us to see where we are and where we are going. It removes uncertain groping and gives us confidence. "Jesus said to the people, 'I am the *Light* of the world. So if you follow me, you won't be stumbling through the darkness, for living light will flood your path.'" (John 8:12b TLB, emphasis added).

Food from heaven is what Jesus called his ministry. He brought food for our starving souls and spirits. "For the *bread of God* is he [Jesus] who comes down from heaven and gives life to the world." (John 6:33 NIV, emphasis added).

Satisfaction presents the good feeling after a feast, when we don't have room for another bite. Jesus is all that our souls can desire.

"Then Jesus declared, 'I am the bread of life. He who comes to me will *never go hungry*, and he who believes in me will *never be thirsty*.'" (John 6:35 NIV, emphasis added).

Clear, flowing spring water is for people whose thirst is desperate. We will never have to look anywhere else for satisfaction. "Jesus answered, 'Everyone who drinks this water will be thirsty again, but whoever drinks the water I give him will never thirst. Indeed, the water I give him will become in him a *spring of water welling up to eternal life*.'" (John 4:13–14 NIV, emphasis added).

Peace or *shalom* pictures the blessing a Hebrew patriarch gives to a child. *Shalom* is much more than the absence of conflict. It is the presence of all of God's blessings. It is wholeness! "*Peace* I leave with you; my peace I give you. I do not give to you as the world gives. Do not let your hearts be troubled and do not be afraid." (John 14:27 NIV, emphasis added).

Imputation pictures charging or crediting an account. We are credited with right standing with God when we place our faith in Jesus. It was not earned; it was given! "Yet he did not waver through unbelief regarding the promise of God, but was strengthened in his faith and gave glory to God, being fully persuaded that God had power to do what he had promised. This is why '*it was credited to him* as righteousness.'" (Rom. 4:20–22 NIV, emphasis added).

Adoption refers to the court proceeding that creates a family, as contrasted with a natural family. "We ourselves, who have the first-fruits of the Spirit, groan inwardly as we wait eagerly for our *adoption* as sons," (Rom. 8:23a NIV, emphasis added).

Sanctification is the process of being made holy and Christ-like. "But you were washed, you were *sanctified*, you were justified in the name of the Lord Jesus Christ and by the Spirit of our God." (1 Cor. 6:11b NIV, emphasis added).

Friend or *confidant* moves away from the Rabbi/disciple mode that the disciples lived in for three years. Can you think of yourself as a "friend" of Jesus? "I no longer call you servants, because a servant does not know his master's business. Instead, I have called you *friends*, for everything that I learned from my Father I have made known to you." (John 15:15 NIV, emphasis added).

Reconciliation pictures two parties totally at odds with each other. In this case our sinfulness has alienated us from God and we want nothing to do with his holiness. But God solved the problem. "All this is from God, who *reconciled* us to himself through Christ and gave us the ministry of *reconciliation*: 19 that God was *reconciling* the world to himself in Christ, not counting men's sins against them." (2 Cor 5:18-19 NIV, emphasis added).

In summary, *salvation* is the amazingly positive relationship we have been given with God when we accept by faith what Jesus has done for us. This is a major part of the Bible. Look at how much time, space, and effort went into explaining this to us. These are pictures of the relationship that *God wants us to understand and to have* with him.

We may look good, behave well, and have a good reputation, but we do not have in ourselves the perfection required for heaven. Jesus offers that to us. It is called salvation.

CHAPTER 41

WHAT DOES *GRACE* MEAN?

"I get tired of people telling jokes about Grace," challenged Jody. "Doesn't everybody know that *grace* is more than a woman's name?"

Phil agreed. "These words that mean more than one thing make good material for humor."

The Bible tells a powerful story about grace. At the end of the story I'll tell you where the grace comes in.

Many Israelites had begun to worship the idols of nearby Canaan. This violated the covenant that Israel had made with God, for God had often pictured their relationship as marriage. At some point in this broken relationship, one of God's prophets heard God speak to him. God told the prophet to get married. His specified bride-to-be was an adulterous woman, unfaithful at the start, just as Israel had been unfaithful to God. The prophet's first child was named Jezreel, meaning "God scatters." Their next child was named Lo-Ruhamah, which means "not pitied." Their next child was named Lo-Ammi, which means "not my people." Can you imagine calling these kids by name for supper? That was God's way of telling his people that they were violating their covenant.

After their third child, the prophet's wife, Gomer, left her husband and children. She returned to her life of prostitution and eventually degenerated to the point that she was sold at the slave market. Her husband's love for her was still so strong that he went to the auction and bought her back. Then he tried to love her back into a faithful relationship.

Did she deserve this love? Certainly not! Even Jesus' teachings allow divorce on the grounds of unfaithfulness. Her unfaithfulness was a lifestyle. But he loved her, even though she did not deserve it. That is *grace*.

Oh, the prophet's name was Hosea.

Many people—or most people, I suppose—would look at Hosea and say, "Man, you are crazy! Certainly you are not going to trust her after what she has done to you!" But what they miss is the fact that Hosea was *acting out how God felt about his people*. This was not a normal human reaction. This was a "God" action.

Grace is hard for most people to grasp. We tend to understand what we have experienced, and most of us have experienced very little grace. What we have learned is "toe the line or pay the consequences." Hosea somehow felt the extreme love that God has, even for his wandering people.

Let me take you back to a parable Jesus told, recorded in Matthew 20. We discussed this is earlier in chapter 31. A landowner hired workers at dawn, midmorning, noon, midafternoon, and one hour before sunset. At the close of the day, the owner, starting with the last one hired, paid each one a denarius, a full day's wage.

Did those who worked only one hour deserve a full day's wage? Certainly not! This is not a story about deserving. This is a parable about grace. What we have trouble getting our heads around is the idea that grace is not about *deserving*. Grace is about *giving*.

Am I saying that God loves us so much that he loves even those who rape, kill, and destroy his creation? Yes. If only they would come to their senses and come home, he would accept them into son-ship as the father did the prodigal son. Jesus said that God yearns for the wandering ones, just as the shepherd searches for his lost sheep.

We humans find it natural to compare ourselves to the people around us. If we keep from running afoul of the law and stay within the moral code of our culture, we consider ourselves "good people." We figure that God ought to see us that way too. What we are missing is that God compares us to *himself*. Uh-oh! Each one of us is compared to perfection. When that happens, we come up short.

God is perfect. His home in heaven is perfect. If I were to get in there, even with my best efforts, I would pollute it. How can I possibly come to God, to heaven? Only by God's grace. It is God's gift that allows the sacrifice of Jesus on the cross of Calvary to pay for our sins. I want to repeat a verse I used earlier: "For it is by *grace* you have been saved, through faith—and this not from yourselves, it is the *gift* of God-" (Eph. 2:8 NIV, emphasis added).

Grace doesn't make much sense to us. We have so little experience with it. It is hard for us to believe it is true. But this is the message of the Christian church from its beginning.

Grace takes something from us. We cannot have the satisfaction of knowing that we earned our position. We cannot have the pride of laying claim to our salvation as our accomplishment. Never can we say that we merit heaven. Every one of us is there only by the grace of God. He gave it to us!

Each one of us is like the lost sheep that has been brought back. Each one of us is like the man who worked only one hour but was paid for a full day. Each one of us is like Gomer, who was rescued from the slave block by the love of Hosea.

Grace is unexpected, undeserved, and hard to believe. It is an awesome gift from an awesome God.

I recommend that you read *What's So Amazing about Grace* by Philip Yancey.

CHAPTER 42

WHAT DID JESUS PREACH/TEACH ABOUT MOST?

"Have you figured out what Jesus meant by 'the kingdom'?" Jody asked Phil.

"No," Phil answered. "Sometimes it seems to be far away. Other times it seems nearby. The pieces of that puzzle don't go together for me either."

I remember as a youth reading the very earliest preaching of Jesus and thinking, *I wonder what that means?* His words were, "Repent, for *the kingdom* of heaven is near," (Matt. 4:17b NIV, emphasis added).

To his listeners, those words were dynamite! They flocked to him. *But I didn't get it!* How were "repent" and "kingdom" related? Even after growing up in the church, attending Sunday school and frequent Bible studies, and listening to hundreds or thousands of sermons, the "kingdom of God" made no sense to me.

After the above Scripture, we read that "Jesus went throughout Galilee, teaching in their synagogues, preaching the good news of *the kingdom*," (Matt. 4:23a NIV, emphasis added). His subject matter was "the kingdom."

The very familiar Sermon on the Mount found in Matthew 5–7 specifically mentions "the kingdom" in two beatitudes and three teachings. In reality, the whole sermon is about "the kingdom." Dallas Willard wrote, "The aim of the sermon—forcefully indicated by its concluding verses—is to help people come to hopeful and realistic terms with their lives here on earth by clarifying, in concrete terms, *the nature of the kingdom* into which they are now invited by Jesus' call."[1]

When Jesus sent the twelve disciples out, they were instructed, "As you go, preach this message: 'The *kingdom* of heaven is near.'" (Matt. 10:7 NIV, emphasis added).

In Jesus' lengthy teaching in Matthew 13, he eleven times said, "*The kingdom* of heaven is is like…(emphasis added)." This whole chapter is a series of word pictures about "the kingdom."

When Jesus was asked about his power to cast out demons, he replied, "But if I drive out demons by the Spirit of God, then *the kingdom* of God has come upon you." (Matt. 12:28 NIV, emphasis added).

Late in his ministry, Jesus gave the disciples authority. "I will give you the keys of *the kingdom* of heaven; whatever you bind on earth will be bound in heaven, and whatever you loose on earth will be loosed in heaven." (Matt. 16:19 NIV).

Jesus taught about the values of "the kingdom" in Matthew 18. We must become as little children to enter the kingdom. If some part of our body makes us sin, I would be better to cut it off rather than miss the kingdom. The shepherd will risk the ninety-nine sheep to hunt for the one that is out of the kingdom. Forgiveness without limit is the kingdom standard.

After the resurrection, Jesus taught, "And this gospel of *the kingdom* will be preached in the whole world as a testimony to all nations, and then the end will come." (Matt. 24:14 NIV, emphasis added).

Finally, Jesus taught that after the final judgment, God would say to the righteous, "'Come, you who are blessed by my Father; take your inheritance, *the kingdom* prepared for you since the creation of the world.'" (Matt. 25:34b NIV, emphasis added).

"The kingdom" is mentioned ninety-three times in the four Gospels—Matthew, Mark, Luke, and John. Obviously, this is the core of Jesus' teachings. But I didn't understand it. Even after growing up in the church and studying the Bible for most of a lifetime, I didn't get it. Are you like me? If I didn't understand something, I just moved on, hoping to find something that did make sense to me. I figured maybe I'd understand it later. But even later, I still did not understand "the kingdom"!

How can we expect to understand the Bible if we do not understand the central teaching of Jesus?

In the next chapter, let's try to understand "the kingdom of heaven," "the kingdom of God." It's so good that we can hardly believe it is true!

I suggest reading *The Divine Conspiracy* by Dallas Willard. This work is very heavy reading, but it's a diamond mine of truth!

CHAPTER 43

WHAT IS THE KINGDOM OF GOD?

"I don't think Americans are interested in the kingdom of God—unless it means heaven," Jody charged. "I don't hear much preaching about it either."

"I don't think I've ever heard a sermon about the kingdom," Phil agreed.

As Americans, we have little time for kings. After all, we had a revolution to break away from George III, the king of England. We are rugged individualists, very comfortable with resisting, even mocking authority. We intend to go our own way and do our own thing. The writer of the symphonic tone poem *An American in Paris* wrote, "*I'll* build a stairway to paradise, with a new step every day. *I'm* going to get there at any price. Step aside, *I'm* on my way!" (emphasis added). The last line of the poem "Invictus" by William Ernest Henley states, "*I am* the master of my fate; *I am* the captain of my soul." (emphasis added). These statements resonate with us, because we have an attitude of self-sufficiency. It has made us a nation of people who "get things done"! We don't expect someone else to do it; *we* do it.

The people of the Bible could not possibly understand us. Every area of their world had a king. They *needed* a king to lead them, to organize their defenses against marauding armies, to plan for natural disasters. When a king died, they rushed to select another king. Life without a king was unthinkable. Their lives were always organized into kingdoms.

So, what is the "kingdom of God"? The kingdom of God is that place where God rules, reigns, and governs.

Just a few moments of thought bring us to realize that God has had a kingdom as long as heaven has existed. We pray in the Lord's Prayer: "Your kingdom come, your will be done on earth *as it is in heaven.*" (Matt. 6:10 NIV, emphasis added). This clearly states that God's will is done perfectly in heaven. Therefore, heaven is part of God's kingdom.

Is there anywhere else that God governs?

"The day is yours, and yours also the night; you established the sun and moon. It was you who set all the boundaries of the earth; you made both summer and winter." (Ps. 74:16–17 NIV). With a little thought, we see that creation gets its order from the Creator. God has placed the stars in their orbits—so precisely that modern humanity has been able to land on the moon and send spaceships to photograph portions of our universe.

What we call "natural laws" are evidence of God's dominion, God's kingship. It appears that our entire universe exists under the rule of God—except for planet Earth! Here, we mortals have been given the freedom to ignore God, actively rebel against God, or choose to live in cooperation with God.

Why would God do that? Because God wanted to expand the love that always existed in the Trinity—God the Father, Son, and Holy Spirit. Certainly he could have created puppets. Puppets are fun, and mechanical pets can be entertaining. But those cute little pieces of machinery *cannot love anyone.*

It's not love unless it is freely given! The only love that is real is a love that can choose to go away. Without that freedom, there is no proof of commitment. It is not really love.

Jesus came to earth, bringing us the opportunity to opt out of the bondage of Satan's kingdom—and opt into God's kingdom. Jesus came with the offer to switch sides, to move from darkness into light, to move from loss to gain, to move from death to life!

In light of this, the kingdom of God did not begin when Jesus came to earth. It has existed for as long as heaven and the created order have existed. Jesus was saying that the kingdom, the rule of God, was now available to all people. No longer would people have to try to be their own god. He would lead them, help them, provide for them, comfort them. He would be their God.

Humanity seems to constantly want to make the kingdom of God a *place* on the map or a set of *external rules* to follow. But Jesus came, teaching that the kingdom was internal, a matter of the heart. "Once, having been asked by the Pharisees when the kingdom of God would come, Jesus replied, 'The kingdom of God does not come with your careful observation, nor will people say, "Here it is," or "There it is," because the kingdom of God is within you.'" (Luke 17:20–21 NIV).

The kingdom of God is a thing of the spirit. Dallas Willard wrote, "The reality of the kingdom life is an inner one, a hidden one, with 'the Father who is in secret.'"[1]

The kingdom of God is *the giving of one's own heart, mind, and spirit to live in harmony with God.* It exists wherever the things that God wants done actually happen! When God's desires are really happening in my life, I am experiencing the kingdom of God—right here, right now!

God's ability to reach down into the lowliest of lives—the poor, the lame, the blind, and the hopeless—is one of the most frequently found themes of the Bible. When John the Baptist sent his followers to question whether Jesus was really the promised Messiah, Jesus responded: "Go back and report to John what you have seen and heard: The blind receive sight, the lame walk, those who have leprosy are cured, the deaf hear, the dead are raised, and the good news is preached to the poor." (Luke 7:22–23 NIV). Right then, Jesus' activities were a demonstration of the kingdom of God!

The kingdom is a *spiritual* reality. It does not exist only in certain places. It does not require government or organization. It does not require physical training or mental accomplishments. It is not limited to academic degrees or financial status. Yet, because it is spiritual, it can exist in all of those places.

The kingdom is a *relationship* that we can choose or reject. When individuals or groups of people choose to trust Jesus as King of their lives, they then experience life on an eternal plane. They have begun to live in "the kingdom." Experiencing the presence and power of Jesus moment by moment in one's life turns it from ordinary living to kingdom living.

The Twenty-third Psalm is the Bible's clearest presentation of that kingdom life. Our little life has been brought into harmony with the Great Shepherd. He leads and directs it!

A.W. Tozer wrote, "The man who has God for his treasure has all things in One."[2]

God yearns to bring us into his kingdom. What we have trouble getting through our heads is that God's intentions for us are always best!

CHAPTER 44

WHAT IS MY KINGDOM?

"Have you ever wondered why so many famous people die so young?" Jody asked.

"Yeah, it seems they burn out," Phil responded. "It must be hard to try to be your own god."

On December 29, 2011, Morgan Freeman, the great actor, was interviewed on the Piers Morgan television show. At one point, Piers asked him, "Are you a man of faith?" Freeman answered, "No! I am God." The subsequent discussion led me to understand that he was not saying he was the Creator but that he was giving control of his life to no one—not even the Creator. I have to wonder if he will hold to that as he nears death. Right now, his fame and fortune have given him the delicious delusion of control.

Morgan Freeman seems to feel that he has a kingdom, and he is its god. That is not wrong. God does intend for each of us to have control over our sphere of influence. Scripture tells us plainly that God created each one of us to "have dominion" over our particular kingdom.

"Then God said, 'Let Us make man in Our image, according to Our likeness; *let them have dominion* over the fish of the sea, over the birds of the air, and over the cattle, over all the earth and over every creeping thing that creeps on the earth.'" (Gen. 1:26 NKJV, emphasis added). "God blessed them and said to them, 'Be fruitful and increase in number; fill the earth and subdue it. *Rule over* the fish of the sea and the birds of the air and over every living creature that moves on the ground.'" (Gen. 1:28 NIV, emphasis added).

"Dominion" and "rule" indicate that each of us has a kingdom. God made us that way! A little consideration will help us see that God intends for each person to have his or her rightful place of influence.

> We have our hairdo, our stance and walk, our particular way of dressing.

> We have our place where we live, with all of those personal touches that make it unique: color, furniture selection, decoration, and knickknacks.

> We have our particular family, with its extended members and various responsibilities.

> We have our friends and associates.

> Many of us have responsibilities for others in our work situation.

> Many of us care for the welfare of plants and animals.

> All of us share in responsibility for the welfare of planet earth.

God has placed us in a very important position!

We need to realize that *God prizes our uniqueness.* Willard wrote, "And there [in the kingdom] God will preserve every one of his treasured friends in the wholeness of their personal existence precisely because he treasures them in that form."[1]

No one else has your exact makeup; each DNA combination is different. No one else has exactly your talents and personality. Only a great God, the Creator of heaven and earth, could come up with this plan that allows him to revel in the unique nature of each human being he has created. God has made us this way, and he delights in our differences. He placed each one of us in our own little kingdom. Each of us has an area of influence!

Not many of us have achieved such accomplishments and fortune that we feel as Morgan Freeman does. Some people seem to fear being swallowed up in the greatness of God, as though they would be lost in God's glory and cease to be! But that is an unfounded fear. Tragically, many of us feel that we have so little value that nobody would miss us if we were swallowed up.

But Jesus taught that in God's eyes we have great value! "So don't be afraid; *you are worth more* than many sparrows." (Matt. 10:31 NIV, emphasis added). "*How much more valuable* is a man than a sheep!" (Matt. 12:12a NIV, emphasis added).

We have been given the right to ignore God, to shake our fists in his face, or to come to him in fellowship and worship. God's plan and purpose is for each one of us who will to join him in his ultimate kingdom.

What an offer! It's better than having a big brother at your back. The Creator-of-all offers to be our heavenly Father. This King can see into the future more clearly than we see into the past. He has all power to defend and provide for his own. He wants us to mature into all that he designed us to become. And his attitude toward us is love. There is no catch to this offer.

Many people spend a lifetime trying to get what God offers for free!

CHAPTER 45

WHAT DOES GOD'S KINGDOM MEAN TO ME?

"Sometimes I think that the kingdom of God is too good to be true," Phil said.

"I know what you mean," Jody responded, "but that's because we've had so much more experience with human kings that let us down. God is another matter entirely."

Can we talk about the kingdom some other way, using other words? Do you remember the Prodigal Son being forgiven and welcomed home by the father? That is what the kingdom means to me.

The father had not been ignoring his son while he was wandering. Instead, the father had been watching for him, eager to protect him from the vengeance of his village. The father would not force the son to change, would not break his will. When the son was ready to come home, his father welcomed him back. It was the son's decision. Also, the father had been making preparations for his son's return, preparing food for a banquet and gala party in honor of the son who would one day come home.

Having been in the "far country" of rebellion against his father, the son finally became aware that he couldn't make it on his own. When he returned, it was not to punishment or probation. He was welcomed into son-ship—immediately. He experienced forgiveness and acceptance—right now.

Inclusion in the family was the father's immediate gift. We are not told of the bath, shampoo, and pedicure, but certainly the father's staff saw that all was provided to get rid of the dirt and smell of the past. Servants do not wear sandals, but the son was given them right away. The best clothing also was provided as a sign of belonging to the father, to the family.

The wealth of the family was immediately available when the father gave his the son the signet ring. In our culture, that would be equivalent to giving him a credit card with no limits. His every need would be supplied by the father. The father's love was not just talk; it was demonstrated.

Being in God's family means being in the kingdom. Being in the kingdom means joy. When a person threw a party like the one mentioned in this parable, the whole village and surrounding area were invited. They feasted joyously for days. Do you remember the mention of the sounds of partying? There was music, and there was dancing—people of all ages in a large circle, dancing jubilantly. And I'll bet there was a lot of animated talking and laughing too.

Being in the kingdom means having purpose, having meaning in life. Now, at last, the prodigal knew who he was. He was a son of the father. The father would lay out the plans for the immediate future, and the family and staff would throw themselves into fulfilling those plans. Now the son could say to himself, "For this reason I was born.

Now I know who I am. Now I know where I am going. I know what I am going to do. I am going to do the will of my father. I am home."

To me, being in the kingdom means that I have a king—not a minor prince from a distant territory but the King of all Kings, the Lord of all Creation. I am not standing alone against the trials and pressures of life. My heavenly Father has made me part of the family. He is intimately involved in my life. Jesus taught that he knows the hairs of my head (not so many anymore). I can go to him at any time or place and know that I have an immediate audience. Even better, I can listen at all times for his guidance and correction. I am not able to see around the corner, but he knows all things and guides me for what is best—in the light of eternity.

All this is possible because of *grace.* The way this world works, little or no grace is ever seen. But in God's kingdom, grace is in the air. Every breath reminds us that God is a *good* God, full of mercy and kindness. How different this is from what we are used to! God knows we are made of dust, but he is constantly trying to draw us to himself with the perfume of his love. And when we come to that nectar, we find *grace.* We find forgiveness, acceptance, belonging, and joy.

Wow! How do we get this? "For it is by grace you have been saved, through faith—and this not from yourselves, it is the gift of God-" (Eph. 2:8 NIV).

The first part of this transaction is God's responsibility. Our part is in the words "through faith." We have to place our trust in Jesus. We have to stop trying to do things on our own. We can never pay for our sins, but Jesus did. He did on Calvary's cross what we could never do for ourselves. He paid the price for our rebellion. Placing our faith in Jesus opens the door to the kingdom. Then God clothes us "in righteousness," places us "in Christ," and accepts us into his kingdom.

The kingdom is that condition where God rules, reigns, and governs.

The kingdom is the giving one's heart, soul, and mind to live in harmony with God.

The kingdom is where the things that God wants done actually happen.

The kingdom of God is his people in his realm living for his purposes.

The kingdom is a relationship with the King that we can accept or reject.

Let's try to summarize this section. You may have heard the saying that we are not all "wired the same." It is absolutely true. Recent findings in neuroscience tell us that the brain develops in the areas of its use. If scrounging for food is our primary activity, the brain will develop to support that activity. Certainly we can see that our daily needs are very different from people of Bible times. Obviously, we will think differently from the way they did. Today we are wired to read, compute, use powerful machinery, and to think medically and psychologically. If we hope to understand the Bible, we need to take into account these differences. We do not think as they did.

But our ultimate needs are exactly the same as theirs. We all need God.

CHAPTER 46

IS REVELATION CONFUSION OR CORONATION?

"The things that happen in Revelation are terrible. I don't even like to think about it. Have you read it?" asked Phil.

Jody responded, "They're not only terrible, the whole thing is totally confusing to me."

Revelation has confounded the greatest of Bible scholars. It is a series of visions that overlap. The sequencing we expect is very difficult, if not impossible, to establish. When reading Revelation, try to look at the big picture. Don't get lost in the details. You will see the church with its problems, Jesus as the coming King, terrible times of judgment of evil, and finally, the end of evil and a new heaven and new earth. God will ultimately make everything right! Look for Jesus. He is the subject of Revelation.

I have one last, big thought about Revelation. There are two major schools of thinking. One says that Revelation was "hope" literature (apocalyptic) for the early church during times of great tribulation. The more popular view now is that it is prophetic literature detailing the end of time. If we look at these views from our comfortable Greek inclinations, we think that one view has to be right and the other wrong. This Greek way says that A can never be B, that an orange can never be an apple. This is excellent logic when applied to Greek material. But Revelation is not Greek. It is very Hebrew. Can we admit for the sake of discussion that God could inspire writing that actually works on several levels—or means different things to different ages?

I believe so.

How about this? Instead of using our familiar Greek approach, let's try the Hebrew way to understand Revelation. First, that would mean that we cannot use the Greek approach that says *we can know all things*. We must be humble about what we can know about God, and be thrilled with whatever he reveals to us. It will be tough, but let's try it.

Next, we cannot insist on what we call *accurate sequencing* of all events. Greeks love accurate sequencing. But Hebrews put things into a sequence that *makes a point*. It is okay for sequence to suffer if the point has been made.

Revelation appears to be a series of overlapping visions. Some scholars list four; others count up to fifteen. Greek thinkers have put much effort into creating an accurate sequence of these segments—with a lot of arguing about which view is correct. From the Hebrew approach, it doesn't matter, as long as *the point has been made*.

Next, Greeks love to use exact words and use them precisely. They like to create an abstract statement that cannot be misunderstood, a statement that can only be seen one way. Hebrews, on the other hand, liked to deliberately paint word pictures that could *be understood on several levels.*

William Barclay wrote, "We must remember that for the devout and scholarly Jew, and especially for the Rabbis, scripture had more than one meaning; and the literal meaning was often regarded as the least important. For the Jewish Rabbis a scripture passage had four meanings. (i) *Pashat,* its simple or literal meaning. (ii) *Remaz,* its suggested meaning. (iii) *Derush,* the meaning deduced by investigation. (iv) *Sod,* the allegorical meaning. The first letters of these words—PRDS—are the consonants of the word *Paradise*—and when a man had succeeded in penetrating into these four different meanings he reached the joy of paradise!"[1]

We can see from William Barclay's statement that it would be totally foreign to the Hebrew mind to believe that one way of thinking, and only one way, can lead to truth. The Hebrews loved God's revelation so much that they looked at it from every angle they could find, so they would not feel that they were doing violence to Revelation to look at it from several different angles.

First of all, it seems obvious to me that Revelation is not a reasoned argument. It is a long series of word pictures, sometimes fantastical pictures.

Second, it makes no pretense to be scientific. It is presenting spiritual truth in picture form. We need to allow our spirits to take in the truth from the giver of ultimate truth, the Holy Spirit, our personal Counselor. That truth may be sensed or understood in avenues other than the highly developed logic our culture uses.

As mentioned above, we must not insist on our way of sequencing things. From our point of view, if something is lacking precise sequence, it cannot be accurate. From their point of view, they are accurate if they have made their point.

And we must allow multiple levels of understanding, which most of us will find very difficult to do.

In practice, what does this mean? It means to look for the big picture without getting lost in the details.

Revelation states its purpose in the first verses. "The revelation of Jesus Christ, which God gave him to show his servants what must soon take place." (Rev. 1:1a NIV). "A revealing of Jesus, the Messiah. God gave it to make plain to his servants what is about to happen." (Rev. 1:1a MSG).

Two reasons are given for the book of Revelation. First, it is about Jesus Christ. Second, it is prophecy about what is soon to happen.

Let's make the first thing the primary thing. What does Revelation say about Jesus? He is much more than the humble carpenter of Nazareth. He is coming in the clouds. He is the Son of Man, who holds the keys to death and hades. He evaluates the seven churches and calls them to purity of purpose.

Then John sees into the future. God's plans are a mystery that no one can solve—except Jesus. In chapter 5, Jesus opens the scroll, revealing God's plans. *Understanding is found only in Jesus.* At the end of the chapter, every creature in heaven and earth falls down to worship Jesus. In chapter 6, there are great troubles.

But chapter 7 says, "Never again will they hunger; never again will they thirst. The sun will not beat upon them, nor any scorching heat. For *the Lamb at the center of the throne will be their shepherd*; he will lead them to springs of living water. And God will wipe away every tear from their eyes" (Rev. 7:16–17 NIV, emphasis added). Again the focus is back on Jesus. He will be "their shepherd."

Chapter 8 through 11:14 are more horrific pictures of great trouble. And then suddenly Jesus reappears. "The seventh angel sounded his trumpet, and there were loud voices in heaven, which said: 'The kingdom of the world has become the kingdom of our Lord and of his Christ, and he will reign for ever and ever.'" (Rev. 11:15 NIV).

Chapter 12 presents a picture of spiritual warfare between God and Satan. God's judgments on evil and Satan follow. Everything about our evil world system is found wanting and is destroyed.

In chapter 19 we again see Jesus. "I saw heaven standing open and there before me was a white horse, whose rider is called Faithful and True. With justice he judges and makes war." (Rev. 19:11 NIV). "On his robe and on his thigh he has this name written: KING OF KINGS AND LORD OF LORDS." (Rev. 19:16 NIV).

Jesus appears again in ultimate authority, as the judge of all humanity. In chapter 20, Satan is chained away from the inhabitants of earth. In chapter 21, we first see a new heaven and new earth. All evil has been removed by the power of the Creator. And the end of the message is this: "I, Jesus, have sent my angel to give you this testimony for the churches. I am the Root and the Offspring of David, and the bright Morning Star." (Rev. 22:16 NIV).

Jesus was saying that he had come from the physical line of David, thus fulfilling ancient prophecy. And he was saying that the fulfillment of the ultimate kingdom was also to be found in him. This is another way of saying that he is all in all, the beginning and the end, the Alpha and the Omega.

Now, let's consider what we just saw. Look at it as a vision or series of visions. This is dream material, not reasoned logic. The message is that *Jesus is Lord*. Jesus is in charge. Jesus will protect. Jesus will be the judge. Jesus will destroy evil, and everything will be made perfect.

Oh, there are terrible pictures of God's wrath and judgment. But that wrath is not on God's children. It is on the followers of Satan.

Revelation is about Jesus. No longer is he the suffering servant of Calvary's hill, but the cosmic King who will end history and rule over the new era of God's kingdom.

Could these pictures apply to the early church? Absolutely. The number 666 fits Nero exactly. (See James M. Efird's *End-Times: Rapture, Antichrist, Miillennium.*[2]) The church at that point was immersed in terrible suffering and persecution. They needed to know that God was still in control.

Could these pictures apply to our day also? Absolutely. As never before in human history, the elements of these pictures appear to apply to our world situation. And increasingly they show what God plans for our world.

But is Revelation about us? No! It is about Jesus.

Revelation shows us how God will demonstrate to believers and nonbelievers alike who Jesus really is. No longer will Jesus be seen as meek and mild. He will be the only one in the world to open the mysteries of God. He will be at the center of the throne of God, acting as his people's Great Shepherd. He will be the King of the kingdom forever. He will be King of all Kings and Lord over all Lords. He will be the promised root and offspring of David, the bright and morning star, the promised one.

Yes, Revelation was *hope* literature for the early church, and I believe it is *prophetic* literature for the end times. Taking this approach allows us to use the Hebrew humility that says that we can know only what God reveals to us. And it allows members of the body of Christ to be more accepting of different understandings. This should draw us together in answer to Jesus' prayer for unity in his body.

Seeing things as "both/and" (the Hebrew way) instead of "either/or" (the Greek way) would solve so many problems in the Christian church. Your understanding is correct (as far as it goes), and so is mine (as far as it goes), my brother. How liberating this Hebrew approach is!

Is Revelation confusing? Not from the Hebrew point of view.

Revelation shows coronation, making Jesus the ultimate King of the ages.

CHAPTER 47

CONCLUSION

The Bible is about God and how he has interacted with his creation. This interaction occurred across 1,500 years in large sections of the Middle East with a very large number of people. God has not hidden himself. To the contrary, he has revealed himself repeatedly and marvelously.

What I am arguing in this book is that we, as Greek thinkers, miss or misunderstand much of the Bible. Why? Because we Greeks/ Westerners do not think as Hebrews did.

The entire Bible was written from a Hebrew mind-set. Because the Hebrews were so close to the earth, their thinking and language was very concrete. They did not have available to them the abstract words we use so easily. We cannot presume that their concrete words say exactly what they seem to mean to us, because they tried to use them to express abstract thoughts. But they could only talk about God in concrete terms.

Most of the Bible was written before what we call logic was available to the writers. So the writers used the Hebrew method of making pictures with words or of telling narratives.

253

Since the Hebrew vocabulary was much smaller than Greek and was much more concrete, they developed techniques to do more with what they had. They learned to use *parallelism*, repeating an idea with other words. They often put the conclusion of a parable in the middle of the teaching, with support all around it.

Of course, they developed their own system of symbols within their community. Their language developed meanings and shades of meanings that we often miss. Naturally, they developed their own idioms in their own language.

So, let's take a quick journey through the discussion of this book.

First, we see the Bible as the written Word of God *if we are open to him*, but it is irrelevant if we reject him. It can only be opened to our spirit by his Spirit.

Too often people try to read the Bible like a novel, and they get bogged down in the Old Testament. It is better seen as a small library or anthology. So, learn to know Jesus first in the Gospels. Then see how the church grew explosively and how problems were solved by calling the believers back to Jesus. Then read the Old Testament as you choose. Finally, read Revelation to find Jesus as the coming King.

Certainly the culture of Bible times can be hard to understand. It was radically different from ours. However, the needs of the human heart are unchanged, and God's answer to our deepest need is still the same.

We have considered the charges that the Bible is illogical and unscientific. Logic, as we know it, was not created until after the Old Testament was finished. The New Testament has logic in some parts but not in others. Of course, the entire Bible was finished before science began with the work of Copernicus. The Bible is not a book of reasoned argument or of science; it is a *spiritual* book. Reasoned argument and science are the wrong tools to try to understand the Bible. It is about God and us, all spiritual beings.

We talked about the expense of writing at that time. Therefore, the writers used an economy of words, only what was necessary to carry the narrative along. We are used to much more detail.

Next, we looked at the worldview of the Hebrew people. We discussed whether all parts, or writing styles, of the Bible are interchangeable, whether all parts apply to our lives today. We presented evidence of the progressing revelation of God, which finally reached its peak when Jesus said, "If you have seen me, you have seen the Father."

Part of the Hebrew worldview involved humility in approaching God and the things of God. They were thrilled at whatever God revealed to them about himself, and they realized that God was far beyond their comprehension. In contrast, the Greeks felt that they could and should understand their gods completely. We must beware of falling into the Greek approach. It is not humble but arrogant.

We discussed Jesus as the heart of the Bible, and the need to approach the reading of the Bible worshipfully. We looked at translations and the big picture of the entire Bible.

We presented Jesus in his role as "the suffering servant" as being central to history. The Bible ultimately is the story of God reaching down into our misery with his healing touch, but that touch required a terrible cost at Calvary.

Next, the language of the Bible can be found in today's modern translation or paraphrase, if that is what you want.

Finally, we discussed the meaning of *salvation*, *grace*, and the *kingdom of God* or *heaven*. Without understanding these terms, the Bible will continue to baffle us.

Of primary importance to me is Jesus' prayer in the gospel of John, chapter 17. There he prayed four times for unity in his body, the church. I feel that our Greek approach to understanding the Bible adds to our failure. Much of the church is separated. We fight over our statements of faith. We do not seem to understand that we are trying to understand Hebrew material with Greek tools. Amazingly, that approach works sometimes, but at other times, it leads us astray.

There are real problems in understanding the Bible. We have presented solutions. Using these tools, which are probably new to us, will not be easy. But if we apply ourselves to understanding our spiritual ancestors, we can understand the Savior that God sent through them. Maybe we can learn to think more with our hearts and less with our logical left brains.

We need to realize that we do not—dare not—worship our statements of faith. They are our best efforts to put into words the faith our hearts hold. But they are words—limited, human, fallible bits of language. To worship them is idolatry. We hold to them because they are the best we can do, but they are not perfect. They are not the Creator. They are not our Redeemer. They are the intellectual framework we use to express what we know about him. Even as we prize them, we need to recognize how imperfect they are.

What we need to desperately hold on to is our Savior and Lord. I experience him a bit differently from the way you do. We should not be surprised at that. We are all different in many ways, so I should not be surprised that you express your understanding in words that are different from mine. But the Savior is the same: one Lord, one faith, one baptism. Let us go together into the future, arm in arm, serving God as revealed through Jesus, united in his love. Maybe then we can fulfill Jesus' prayer for the unity of his body and become what he wants us to be: his people, united in his service in his kingdom.

The Bible is our sourcebook. It is the God-inspired, God-preserved record of his coming into our human history. Ultimately, is it God's touch of our spirit by his Spirit.

NOTES

Chapter 1

1. Willard, Dallas. *Hearing God*, (Downers Grove, Ill.: InterVarsity Press, 1999), 65.
2. Sproul, Robert C. *Knowing Scripture*, revised edition, (Downers Grove, Ill.: InterVarsity Press, 2009), 21.
3. Luther, Martin. In *The Spiritual Formation Bible, New Revised Standard Version*, (Grand Rapids, Mich.: Zondervan Publishing House, 1999), 927.
4. Tozer, Aiden W. *The Knowledge of the Holy*, (New York: HarperOne, 1961). 65.
5. Law, William. A Serious Call to a Devout and Holy Life, In *The Spiritual Formation Bible, New Revised Standard Version*, (Grand Rapids, Mich.: Zondervan Publishing House, 1999), 671.

Chapter 2

1. Sproul, Robert C. *Knowing Scripture*, revised edition, (Downers Grove, Ill.: InterVarsity Press, 2009), 132.

Chapter 5

1. Orr, James. *The International Standard Bible Encyclopaedia*. In *PC Study Bible 5.0F, Complete Reference Library*. (Seattle, Washington, Biblesoft, Inc. 2008). s.v. "Centurion".

2. Barclay, William. *The Daily Study Bible Series, Matthew, Revised Edition.* (Philadelphia: The Westminster Press, 1975). Volume 1, 168.

Chapter 6

1. Keener, Craig S. *IVP Bible Background Commentary*, In *PC Study Bible 5.0F, Complete Reference Library.* (Seattle, Washington, Biblesoft, Inc. 2008). s.v. "Luke 19:8".

Chapter 7

1. Keener, Craig S. *IVP Bible Background Commentary*, In *PC Study Bible 5. 0F, Complete Reference Library.* (Seattle, Washington, Biblesoft, Inc. 2008). s.v. "Matthew 27:26".
2. Gray, Henry. *Gray's Anatomy, Twenty-Seventh Edition*, Goss, Charles Mayo, editor. (Philadelphia, Lee and Febiger, 1959). 1022, 1024.
3. Barclay, William. *The Daily Study Bible Series, Matthew, Revised Edition.* (Philadelphia: The Westminster Press, 1975). Volume 1, 395.

Chapter 8

1. Youngblood, Ronald F. *Nelson's Illustrated Bible Dictionary*, In *PC Study Bible 5.0F, Complete Reference Library.* (Seattle, Washington, Biblesoft, Inc. 2008). s.v. "Eunuch".

Chapter 10

1. Unger, Merrill F., *The New Unger's Bible Dictionary*, In *PC Study Bible 5.0F, Complete Reference Library.* (Seattle, Washington, Biblesoft, Inc. 2008). s.v. "Syrophoenician".

Chapter 11

1. Youngblood, Ronald F., *Nelson's Illustrated Bible Dictionary*, In *PC Study Bible 5.0F, Complete Reference Library*. (Seattle, Washington, Biblesoft, Inc. 2008). s.v. "Pharisee".
2. Youngblood, Ronald F., *Nelson's Illustrated Bible Dictionary*, In *PC Study Bible 5.0F, Complete Reference Library*. (Seattle, Washington, Biblesoft, Inc. 2008). s.v."Scribes".
3. Barclay, William. *The Daily Study Bible Series: Matthew, Revised Edition*. (Philadelphia: The Westminster Press, 1975). Volume 1, 128.
4. Youngblood, Ronald F. *Nelson's Illustrated Bible Dictionary*, In *PC Study 5.0F, Complete Reference Library*. (Seattle, Washington, Biblesoft, Inc. 2008). s.v."Sadducees".
5. Youngblood, Ronald F. *Nelson's Illustrated Bible Dictionary*, In *PC Study Bible 5.0F, Complete Reference Library*. (Seattle, Washington, Biblesoft, Inc. 2008). s.v."Levites".
6. Youngblood, Ronald F. *Nelson's Illustrated Bible Dictionary*, In *PC Study Bible 5. 0F, Complete Reference Library*. (Seattle, Washington, Biblesoft, Inc. 2008). s.v. "Herodians".
7. Youngblood, Ronald F. *Nelson's Illustrated Bible Dictionary*, In *PC Study Bible 5.0F, Complete Reference Library*. (Seattle, Washington, Biblesoft, Inc. 2008). s.v. "Zealots".

Chapter 13

1. Tackett, Del. *The Truth Project*, Focus on the Family. www.focusonthefamily.com (Accessed 1-11-14)

Chapter 14

1. Youngblood, Ronald F. *Nelson's Bible Dictionary,* In *PC Study Bible 5. 0F, Complete Reference Library*. (Seattle, Washington, Biblesoft, Inc. 2008). s.vv."Diseases, Leprosy".

Chapter 16

1. Barclay, William. *The Daily Study Bible Series: Matthew, Revised Edition.* (Philadelphia: The Westminster Press, 1975). Volume 1, 129–130.
2. Youngblood, Ronald F. *Nelson's Illustrated Bible Dictionary,* In *PC Study Bible 5. 0F, Complete Reference Library.* (Seattle, Washington, Biblesoft, Inc. 2008). s.v. "Corban".

Chapter 21

1. Keener, Craig S. *IVP Bible Background Commentary,* In *PC Study Bible 5. 0F, Complete Reference Library.* (Seattle, Washington, Biblesoft, Inc. 2008). s.v. "Matthew 1:17".
2. Keener, Craig S. *IVP Bible Background Commentary,* In *PC Study Bible 5. 0F, Complete Reference Library.* (Seattle, Washington, Biblesoft, Inc. 2008). s.v. "Luke 3:23".
3. Ryken, Leland. *Dictionary of Biblical Imagery,* (Downers Grove, Ill., InterVarsity Press, 1998). s.v. "Forty", 305.

Chapter 22

1. Efird, James M. *End-Times, Rapture, Antichrist, Millennium.* (Nashville, Tenn.: Abingdon Press, 1986). 39.
2. Vine, William E. *Vine's Expository Dictionary of Biblical Words,* In *PC Study Bible 5.0F, Complete Reference Library.* (Seattle, Washington, Biblesoft, Inc. 2008). s.vv. "Ever, Forever".

Chapter 23

1. Ryken, Leland. *Dictionary of Biblical Imagery,* (Downers Grove, Ill., InterVarsity Press, 1998). xiv.

2. Essig, Montgomery F. *The Comprehensive Analysis of the Bible.* (Nashville, Tenn., The Southwestern Company, 1951). 593–595.

Chapter 24

1. Leman, Wayne. "Hebrew Bible Idioms and Other Figures of Speech." *www.bible-translation.110mb.com/otidioms.htm* (Accessed 1-03-14)
2. Miller, Dave. "Bible Idioms: Did You Mean What I Think You Said?" Discovery Magazine, 5-2-2011, Apologetics Press. *www.apologeticspress.org/apPubPage.aspx?pub=2&issue=971&article=1490* (Accessed 1-03-14)
3. Keener, Craig S. *IVP Bible Background Commentary*, In *PC Study Bible 5.0F, Complete Reference Library.* Seattle, Washington, Biblesoft, Inc. 2008. s.v. "John 6:63".
4. Wiersbe, Warren W. *The Bible Exposition Commentary*, In *PC Study Bible 5.0F, Complete Reference Library.* Seattle, Washington, Biblesoft, Inc. 2008. s.v. "John 6:63".
5. Lamsa, George M. *Idioms in the Bible Explained and A Key to the Original Gospels.* (San Francisco, Harper and Row, Publishers, 1985). 54.
6. Bullinger, E. W. *Figures of Speech Used in the Bible*, (Grand Rapids, Mich., Baker Book House, reprinted 1968). 846.
7. Ryken, Leland. *Dictionary of Biblical Imagery*, (Downers Grove, Ill., InterVarsity Press, 1998). 305.

Chapter 25

1. Bailey, Kenneth. *Jesus through Middle Eastern Eyes.* (Downer's Grove, Ill.: IVP Academic, InterVarsity Press, 2008). 353-354.
2. Ryken, Leland. *Dictionary of Biblical Imagery*, (Downers Grove, Ill., InterVarsity Press, 1998). 955.

3. Sire, James. *How to Read Slowly*, (Colorado Springs, Colo.: WaterBrook Press, 1978). 46.

Chapter 26

1. Jeffrey, Grant. "Startling Archeological Discoveries.", The Signature of God, *Prophecy on Line, www.grantjeffrey.com/ article/article7.htm* (Accessed 1-03-14)
2. Ibid.

Chapter 27

1. Sire, James. *How to Read Slowly*, (Colorado Springs, Colo.: WaterBrook Press, 1978). 184.
2. Ryken, Leland. *Dictionary of Biblical Imagery*, (Downers Grove, Ill., InterVarsity Press, 1998). xiii.
3. Ibid.

Chapter 28

1. Sproul, Robert C. *Knowing Scripture*, revised edition, (Downers Grove, Ill.: InterVarsity Press, 2009), 115.
2. Ryken, Leland. *Dictionary of Biblical Imagery*, (Downers Grove, Ill., InterVarsity Press, 1998). xx.
3. Ibid.

Chapter 29

1. Ryken, Leland. *Dictionary of Biblical Imagery*, (Downers Grove, Ill., InterVarsity Press, 1998). xiii.

Chapter 30

1. Tackett, Del. *The Truth Project*. (Focus on the Family Institute, 1997). www.focusonthefamily.com. (Accessed 1-3-14)

Chapter 31

1. Bailey, Kenneth. *Jesus through Middle Eastern Eyes.* (Downer's Grove, Ill.: IVP Academic, InterVarsity Press, 2008). 279-354.

Chapter 34

1. Willard, Dallas. *Hearing God.* (Downers Grove, Ill.: InterVarsity Press, 1999). 127.

Chapter 36

1. Youngblood, Ronald F., *Nelson's Illustrated Bible Dictionary*, In *PC Study 5.0F, Complete Reference Library.* (Seattle, Washington, Biblesoft, Inc. 2008). s.v."Isaiah".
2. Youngblood, Ronald F., *Nelson's Illustrated Bible Dictionary*, In *PC Study Bible 5.0F, Complete Reference Library.* (Seattle, Washington, Biblesoft, Inc. 2008). s.v."David".

Chapter 37

1. Nicolson, Adam. "The King James Bible, Making a Masterpiece," Volume 220, Number 6, *National Geographic* (December 2011): 43.
2. Sproul, Robert C. *Knowing Scripture*, (Downers Grove, Ill.: InterVarsity Press, 2009). 132.

Chapter 38

1. Ryken, Leland. *Dictionary of Biblical Imagery*, (Downers Grove, Ill., InterVarsity Press, 1998). 447.
2. Council of Nicaea. In *PC Study Bible 5.0F, Complete Reference Library.* (Seattle, Washington, Biblesoft, Inc. 2008). s.vv. "Creeds of the Church".

3. Council of Chalcedon. In *PC Study Bible 5.0F, Complete Reference Library.* (Seattle, Washington, Biblesoft, Inc. 2008). s.vv. "Creeds of the Church".

Chapter 39

1. Lucado, Max. *No Wonder They Call Him the Savior,* (Seattle: Multnomah Press, 1986). 11.
2. Lucado, Max. *Six Hours One Friday,* (Seattle: Multnomah Books, 1989). 73.
3. Catherine of Siena, In *The Spiritual Formation Bible, New Revised Standard Version.* (Grand Rapids, Mich.: Zondervan Publishing House, 1999). 1246.

Chapter 40

1. Ryken, Leland. *Dictionary of Biblical Imagery,* (Downers Grove, Ill., InterVarsity Press, 1998). 421.
2. Ibid., 448.

Chapter 42

1. Willard, Dallas. *The Divine Conspiracy,* (San Francisco: Harper, 1997). 133.

Chapter 43

1. Willard, Dallas. *The Divine Conspiracy,* (San Francisco: Harper, 1997). 279.
2. Tozer, Aiden W. *The Pursuit of God,* (Camp Hill, Pa.: Christian Publications, 1982). 19.

Chapter 44

1. Willard, Dallas. *The Divine Conspiracy*, (San Francisco: Harper, 1997). 85.

Chapter 46

1. Barclay, William. *The Daily Bible Study Series: Galatians, Revised Edition*. (Philadelphia: The Westminster Press, 1975). 40–41.
2. Efird, James M. *End-Times, Rapture, Antichrist, Millennium*, (Nashville, Tenn.: Abingdon Press, 1986). 66–67.

SOURCES

Bailey, Kenneth E. *Jesus through Middle Eastern Eyes.* Downer's Grove, Ill.: IVP Academic, InterVarsity Press, 2008.

Barclay, William. *The Daily Study Bible Series, Revised Edition.* Philadelphia: The Westminster Press, 1975.

Bullinger, E. W. *Figures of Speech Used in the Bible.* Grand Rapids, Mich.: Baker Book House, reprinted 1968.

Efird, James M. *End-Times, Rapture, Antichrist, Millennium.* Nashville, Tenn.: Abingdon Press, 1986.

Essig, Montgomery F., *The Comprehensive Analysis of the Bible.* Nashville, Tenn., The Southwestern Company, 1951.

Goss, Charles M. *Grey's Anatomy.* Philadelphia: Lea and Febiger, 1959.

Jeffrey, Grant. "Startling Archeological Discoveries.", The Signature of God, *Prophecy on Line, www.grantjeffrey.com/article/article7.htm* (Accessed 1-03-14)

Keener, Craig S. *IVP Bible Background Commentary: New Testament.* In *PC Study Bible 5.0F, Complete Reference Library.* Seattle, Washington, Biblesoft, Inc. 2008.

Keller, Timothy. *The Reason for God: Belief in an Age of Skepticism.* New York: Dutton, 2008.

Lamsa, George M. *Idioms in the Bible Explained and A Key to the Original Gospels.* San Francisco, Harper and Row, Publishers, 1985.

Leman, Wayne. "Hebrew Bible Idioms and Other Figures of Speech." *www.bible-translation.110mb.com/otidioms.htm* (Accessed 1-03-14)

Lucado, Max. *No Wonder They Call Him the Savior.* Seattle: Multnomah Press, 1986.

Lucado, Max. *Six Hours One Friday.* Seattle: Multnomah Books, 1989.

Miller, Dave. "Bible Idioms: Did You Mean What I Think You Said?" Discovery Magazine, 5-2-2011, Apologetics Press. *www.apologeticspress.org/apPubPage.aspx?pub=2&issue=971&article=1490* (Accessed 1-03-14)

Nicolson, Adam. "The King James Bible, Making a Masterpiece," Volume 220, Number 6, *National Geographic,* December 2011

Orr, James, *The International Standard Bible Encyclopaedia.* In *PC Study Bible 5.0F, Complete Reference Library.* Seattle, Washington, Biblesoft, Inc. 2008.

Ryken, Leland, et al. *The Dictionary of Biblical Imagery.* Downer's Grove, Ill.: InterVarsity Press, 1998.

Sire, James. *How to Read Slowly.* Colorado Springs, Colo.: WaterBrook Press, 1978.

Sproul, Robert C. *Knowing Scripture,* Downers Grove, Ill.: InterVarsity Press, 2009.

Tackett, Del. *The Truth Project.* Focus on the Family Institute, 1997, www.focusonthefamily.com. (Accessed 1-3-14)

The Spiritual Formation Bible, New Revised Standard Version. Grand Rapids, Mich.: Zondervan Publishing House, 1999.

Tozer, A. W. *The Knowledge of the Holy.* New York: HarperOne, 1961.

Tozer, A. W. *The Pursuit of God.* Camp Hill, Pa.: Christian Publications, 1982.

Unger, Merrill F., *The New Unger's Bible Dictionary.* In *PC Study Bible 5.0F, Complete Reference Library.* Seattle, Washington, Biblesoft, Inc. 2008.

Wiersbe, Warren W. *The Bible Exposition Commentary.* In *PC Study Bible5.0F, Complete Reference Library.* Seattle, Washington, Biblesoft, Inc. 2008.

Willard, Dallas. *Hearing God.* Downers Grove, Ill.: InterVarsity Press, 1999.

Willard, Dallas. *The Divine Conspiracy.* San Francisco: Harper, 1997.

Yancey, Philip. *What's so Amazing about Grace?* Grand Rapids, Mich. Zondervan Publishing House, 1997.

Youngblood, Ronald F., *Nelson's Illustrated Bible Dictionary*, In *PC Study Bible 5.0F, Complete Reference Library.* Seattle, Washington, Biblesoft, Inc. 2008.

ABBREVIATIONS

AB   Amplified Bible

BBE   Bible in Basic English

KJV   King James Version

MSG   The Message

NASB   New American Standard Bible

NET   New English Translation

NIV   New International Version

NKJV   New King James Version

NLT   New Living Translation

TLB   The Living Bible

YLT   Young's Literal Translation

The author can be contacted at:

Clarence Whetstone

PO Box 182

Bedford, PA 15522

Or at the website: www.cwhetstone.com

ABOUT THE AUTHOR

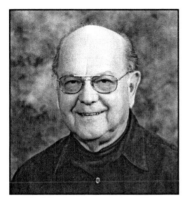

I have been immersed in the Bible from my mother's knee. As a preacher's kid, I was required to attend Sunday School, Bible studies, Bible conferences, etc. all my junior years. Being expected to follow my father's vocation, I started ministerial training and was licensed as a local preacher. I held three small churches during my college years and had one year of seminary before leaving the ministerial training track. During my nine and half years of higher education, I amassed majors in English, theology, psychology and speech therapy. In recent years I have felt compelled to write material above.

My career has been spent in speech therapy, in Blair and Bedford Counties, PA, primarily in the school system. I still work part-time with a local nursing service.

My wife and I live near Bedford, PA. We have been actively involved in the local church since 1960 and presently lead a large adult Sunday School class. Across the years I have been invited to speak in over one hundred different venues. I also sing and play trombone in a gospel band called Heaven Bound which ministers in local churches and events. My other interests have always been the visual arts, expressed in photography and painting.

CPSIA information can be obtained at www.ICGtesting.com
Printed in the USA
BVOW03s2143060514

716BV00001B/4/P

9 781490 827193